How to Raise a Conservative Daughter

HOW TO RAISE A CONSERVATIVE DAUGHTER

MICHELLE EASTON

Regnery
1947 | 75 YEARS | 2022
WASHINGTON, D.C.

ISBN: 978-1-68451-334-5
Library of Congress Control Number: 2021936545

First trade paperback edition published 2022

Published in the United States by
Regnery Publishing
A Division of Salem Media Group
Washington, D.C.
www.Regnery.com

Manufactured in the United States of America

10 9 8 7 6 5 4 3 2 1

This book is dedicated to my daughter Shelley, who inspires my work every day, and to my granddaughter Josephine, who has my hopes for a bright future

CONTENTS

Introduction

Like every parent, you cherish that sweet and wondrous moment when you hold your child in your arms for the very first time. A wave of emotion washes over you. Joy. Gratitude. Humility. Hope. You experience it all. Then, after weeks of sleepless nights, crying, feeding, and diaper changes, the rigorous demands of parenting set in. This tiny, precious life—a blessing from God—is dependent on you to protect, provide, and teach him or her life's lessons. And if that bundle of joy is a little girl, the challenges that lie ahead are quite daunting.

Raising a daughter is hard enough. Raising a *conservative* daughter can seem downright impossible. If we're honest, some days are so hectic that we struggle just to get our child to school with her homework done, a bite to eat for lunch, and matching socks on her feet. When moms and dads do have time to ponder their daughter's long-term values, many assume she will soak them up from family along the way.

Our family has always supported conservative principles, and our kids will do the same.

We come from a military family, so our children will naturally be patriotic.

We sent our daughter to an expensive private school, so she won't fall for all that Leftist nonsense in college.

On and on it goes. All of these thoughts seem reasonable. But unfortunately, all too often that's just not how things turn out.

I hear the same complaint all the time from parents who feel confused and defeated.

"We don't know what happened," they tell me with pain in their voices. "We gave her every tool, every advantage…and yet one day we looked up and realized our little girl had grown up and rejected our family's traditional values and beliefs. What happened? Where did we go wrong?"

My heart goes out to these families. Truly. As someone who has spent more than a quarter century training thousands of conservative girls and women for effective leadership, I empathize with the high hurdles parents face. Working with all these young women and observing more parents and families than most, I've developed great appreciation and understanding of what parents and families can do to raise a conservative daughter in an increasingly hostile environment.

Toxic social media, radical feminist indoctrination in schools, corrosive messages from Hollywood and the entertainment world, a Leftist media that stokes radical anti-American movements—the dizzying array of cultural forces aligned against families is real and immediate. But so are the remedies.

Here's the core issue: often, parents either don't know what to do or don't do what they know. Put another way, it's all about instilling the right "pillars" of belief—core conservative values and ideas—in your daughter and then strengthening those beliefs through practical, consistent, real-life application. The trick is knowing which pillars to instill and the best ways to teach them. And that's where many parents hit a wall.

A big part of the challenge to conservative parenting is that there are limited resources on the topic. We have mountains of quality books on pregnancy, childhood discipline, pediatric health, spiritual development, and education. But there is relatively little on instilling conservative values, much less for daughters. That leaves moms and dads to experiment as they go and hope for the best. Some parents will point out an important conservative concept (such as limited government or the pro-life position) to their daughter as if they are pointing to a star in the sky. But unless they explain how that "star" connects to those around it, she is unable to see and internalize the bigger "constellation" of conservative meaning they're trying to teach her. This book explains the most important "stars" and how to connect them into meaningful "constellations" through engaging experiences and conversations.

To be sure, there are no guarantees, no magic pills. But there are proven and sometimes counterintuitive techniques moms and dads can use to significantly increase the odds that their girl will hold fast to traditional values. The secret is learning how to translate conservative principles into lessons, language, and experiences your daughter can understand, relate to, and retain. If that sounds like a tall order, that's because it is. I should know.

I wrote *How to Raise a Conservative Daughter* to share with parents the pearls of wisdom I've collected over a lifetime spent in the conservative movement equipping the next generation of female leaders. After receiving presidential appointments from Presidents Ronald Reagan and George H. W. Bush to serve at the U.S. Department of Education and also working for them at several other departments for the full twelve years of their administrations, I realized there was a need for an organization that could mentor and support conservative girls and women. In 1993, I founded the Clare Boothe Luce Center for Conservative Women. Now, nearly three decades later, our thousands of alumnae serve on the frontlines in promoting constitutional principles such as individual freedom, economic liberty, limited government, pro-life causes, and traditional values at the local, state, and federal levels. As wives and mothers, these women are now passing conservatism on to their children.

My hope is that the principles and practical tools this book provides will help you and your family raise smart, fun, conservative daughters. I've purposely written this book for you to use at any stage of your daughter's development. If you're a soon-to-be parent, reading and thinking about these concepts early on will give you time to consider how you will introduce conservativism to your daughter in the years ahead. If your girl is already a teenager, or even in college, this book will give you ways to spark thought-provoking conversations—and to challenge the Leftist propaganda she's being taught or exposed to in high school or college.

Because every girl is unique, you should feel free to customize and modify these lessons. After all, there's no such thing as a perfect way to parent a conservative daughter. So relax. Pour yourself some coffee, grab a pen to jot some notes, and find a quiet spot to read (or as quiet a place as any busy parent can realistically hope to find). My goal is to get you thinking about those core conservative pillars and how to instill them to strengthen and support your girl's heart and mind. If you do that, you will have given your daughter a priceless and enduring gift.

As my old boss President Ronald Reagan once said, "Freedom is never more than one generation away from extinction. We didn't pass it to our children in the bloodstream. It must be fought for, protected, and handed on for them to do the same."

As with so much else, President Reagan was right. Our children won't grow up to be conservatives by magic or osmosis, especially in today's cultural climate. Conservative beliefs must be taught, nurtured, and cultivated throughout a girl's upbringing. As parents, we have the privilege of doing the teaching. Cherish and enjoy that challenge. Few things in life are more important.

CHAPTER 1

Self-Worth Flows from God, Not Government

The greatest gift parents can give their daughter is the knowledge that she is uniquely made and unconditionally loved by God. When a girl knows that the Creator of the universe cares deeply about her problems, hopes, and challenges, she learns that her self-worth is rooted in things far greater than what the world tells her. She realizes she is special, cared for, and eternally valued; that she is a child of God. It will give her an inner power like no other.

When I was growing up as a shy, middle-class girl in Rye, New York, my parents took me to church regularly. It was just what you did in those days. My parents weren't religious zealots. Nor were they particularly vocal about their Christian beliefs. But they believed the church offered moral direction and wholesome friendships. They thought of church as a place where I could learn the virtues and values contained in the Bible. They were right, and I'm glad they brought me.

As a young girl sitting in the church pews, I didn't understand the connection between faith and freedom. I'm not sure my parents did either. But as I grew and studied history, I discovered one of the core principles of conservatism: religious faith and human freedom are inextricably linked.

Have you ever wondered why totalitarian and tyrannical governments impose atheism on their people? The reason is that people who believe in God believe in an eternal afterlife—and people who believe in an eternal afterlife are dangerous. They are bold, courageous, and not afraid to sacrifice themselves for causes bigger than themselves. People of faith believe that their self-worth comes from God, not government. No dictator can tolerate people with that kind of confidence and conviction. It threatens their control and power. As history has shown, tyrannical governments have tortured, beaten, imprisoned, executed, and annihilated people of faith in an attempt to crush freedom movements and enforce atheism.

Governmental hostility to faith doesn't always involve sanctioned atheism or killing. Modern socialism, for example, fosters government dependency. In the United States, government dependency teaches girls that their self-worth comes from food stamps, abortion clinics, and their secular education. The Left's message to our daughters is that minimum wage, lousy health care, public housing, and a little walking-around cash assistance is the best they can hope for. Worse, it teaches that government is their higher power and politics is a stand-in for religion. Our daughters deserve so much better!

It's true that people often need a hand up for legitimate reasons, and they deserve compassion and support. Any one of us could be in that position one day. But consigning a girl's initiative and her self-worth to a lifetime of government programs is soul-crushing. It will never deliver happiness and prosperity. It will never unleash your daughter's potential. It will never be enough to fill the human void. Uncle Sam is not a worthy substitute for a good father and graceful mother, much less God.

The growth of government, along with a politicized education system, has eroded old taboos. There are plenty of studies showing how women can receive the equivalent of a middle-class income in public benefits if they get pregnant, have kids, and don't marry.[1] The message to our girls: rely on government, not God. It's a soulless trap. "Free" will always be tempting, and it creates incentives for girls to make harmful decisions. As parents we need to guard our children and provide for them, otherwise government and society will. How do parents do this? By instilling that self-worth flows from God, not government.

What Is Self-Worth?

Put simply, self-worth is a deep understanding of one's value as a human being. It's your inner sense of importance. It can be positive or negative, and it varies by degree. But there's no greater source of self-worth than God.

The great conservative thinker and author William F. Buckley once said that it is hard for a person who does not believe in God to be a conservative. It's not impossible, of course, but Buckley's insight confirms what I've seen in the lives of many, many girls. I've had the pleasure to work with thousands of young women over the years and have seen how their faith sustains them. Belief in God gives them a sense of purpose. Faith is foundational to freedom. Without faith, girls often fall victim to what the government, their peers, and pop culture say they are worth.

Self-worth is a deeply conservative concept that places the value of the individual outside of the reach of cultural forces and government. But Leftists have tried to undermine the robust conception of self-worth by replacing it with self-esteem.

While self-worth establishes freedom by liberating the individual from the vicissitudes of the moment, self-esteem, a mere feeling, chains people to the pathologies of their time. Self-esteem makes fragile people who look to others for validation. According to the Left, self-esteem is the most important thing for children. Self-esteem can certainly be positive, but praising children for fear of hurting their feelings is a poor substitute for nurturing their true, innate value as children of a loving God.

The "participation-trophy" approach that permeates schools creates a fragile confidence that has no true foundation. Self-worth, on the other hand, puts people in touch with something much bigger and more important. You don't need validation or approval from others when you know you are unconditionally loved by a holy God.

Government can't build self-worth. Why? Because governments are made of people, and people are fallible. The best government can do is reflect the people that run it. Leaving morality and ethics up to government is a losing proposition from the start because you are relying on people as opposed to God. Ask yourself: Do you really want to outsource your daughter's moral code to politicians and bureaucrats?

Think about some of the things governments have done, like condoning slavery and the Dred Scott decision. Think about the U.S. Supreme Court's decision on abortion and how it has led to the destruction of 60 million innocent babies' lives. Government and popular culture think that's just fine, and they even celebrate it. The German government once systematically annihilated 6 million Jews and anyone who didn't agree with its horrific ideology. Communist and totalitarian governments have killed an estimated 100 million people. The atrocities at the hands of tyrannical governments are commonplace.

Religion frees people from the moral judgments of their day. It gives them the moral authority to assess whether their society has been led astray. Of course, you do not have to be religious to understand that you are uniquely created and that you have a higher purpose. But it sure helps.

Take Your Daughters to Church

If you want your daughter to understand her self-worth, she has to know its source. Since self-worth flows from something larger than oneself, why not expose her to the greatest knowable source of love and purpose imaginable? It's not school, celebrity, or Instagram. The answer is God. And faith is nurtured in houses of worship.

You don't have to be the most devout person to experience the benefits of worship. Spiritual development can be a huge addition to your girl's life. At a minimum, where would you rather have your daughter meet friends or, dare we say, a boy? Where better to find affirmation against the type of peer pressure that too often leads to destructive teenage behavior?

Churches and synagogues teach girls to appreciate that there is more out there than worldly desires. Girls can find healthy role models and forge thoughtful friendships with other families. They need faithful mentors and friends they can rely on, in addition to learning about their higher calling. All of that is built into the fabric of faith communities.

There's an old joke that if children don't go to church, then they can't rebel against their faith when they go to college. Like all good humor, there's some truth to it. The key, however, is to plant the seeds when they're young. *Train up a child in the way he should go: and when he is old, he will not depart from it* (Proverbs 22:6).

I've listened to many young women offer their thoughts about faith and belief. Often, their parents would take them to church when they were girls, then they would stop going when they were older. But at some point, they found their way back to faith. Consider this testimony from a Luce Center college intern: "Once my grandma passed away, we never found ourselves back in church. But the memories I have from the early Sunday school services and Vacation Bible School, those were formative."

You learn it. You leave it. You come back to it. That's the path many take when it comes to faith. But it begins at home. What could be more wonderful than your daughter's knowing deep in her heart that she's uniquely created and that God has a purpose and a plan for her that involves hope and prosperity, not harm? Children need to be immersed in a community of faith to understand that, and if you plant the seeds when they are young, they are more likely to take root and provide a foundation for true self-worth. It isn't just about attending weekly church or synagogue services. It's saying grace at meals. It's celebrating baptisms, communions, ordinations, and other religious observations.

Government can never replace God. Flawed human beings are no substitute for a loving relationship with our Creator. Take your daughter to church. Encourage her spiritual growth. Sometimes a loving nudge from a parent or grandparent is all it takes to bestow the blessings of faith. Never underestimate your influence when daughters are young or when they are older and have their own families.

Don't Give Your Daughter a Participation Trophy; Give Her the Truth

There's a fallacy that adults constantly need to inflate a child's self-esteem or else the child is at risk of veering off course. This impulse may be well-intended, but it's misguided. Children, especially girls, are much tougher and more durable than what government and modern "helicopter parents" realize. The problem is most apparent in public schools, where every student gets a proverbial trophy, and there are no losers. Tag and dodgeball are out; subjective grading is in. Competition is viewed as evil, masculine, and rooted in capitalism. Failing is all but forbidden for fear of hurt feelings. Everyone's a winner, the liberal logic goes, even though we all know that's not the truth.

What is this teaching our girls? I would argue that it's actually ensuring failure. Girls who are not allowed to fail become ill-equipped to deal with adversity. Losing and mistakes are a part of life. Overcoming obstacles through hard work and perseverance builds character and authentic self-worth and confidence, rather than a cheapened self-esteem "sugar high."

When girls are conditioned to believe that everything they do is a success, it sets them up to struggle later in life. Trouble keeping up in college? Time for an "emotional support animal" and a "safe space." Feelings get hurt? Run to the nearest "crying circle." Experiencing professional and financial hardships at the outset of a career? Obviously it's sexism that only government can fix.

One doesn't need to jump to extreme conclusions to realize the harm of universal trophy culture. It's so important for parents to be honest with their daughters. My sister understands this concept well. She taught children in Cape Cod schools for many years, and the teachers were instructed to tell each child how awesome they were several times a day. "But they weren't awesome," she once confided in me. "Certainly not as often as we were supposed to tell them."

So, what did she do? She told the truth. When the children deserved praise, she said so. When they didn't, she respected them enough not to mislead them. Eventually, unearned praise becomes meaningless when children hear it so much. Kids are smart; they know when adulation is deserved and when it's puffery. The solution is selective, loving reinforcement based on reality, not phony emotional manipulation. It builds true confidence and self-worth.

Loving reinforcement doesn't mean shredding an eight-year-old's painting or poem as if you're the culture critic at the *New York Times*. It means finding something that you like and reinforcing it. "This is a great color here," or, "I like this phrase you used, but here's what I would do to make it even better." You're neither falsely praising nor abusing her vulnerability; you're being honest and helping your daughter grow.

Teach Modesty

Teach your daughter modesty. It may not always be cool, but it's absolutely a virtue—and that goes for boys and girls. Immodest choices invite all manner of headaches and heartaches, and you don't have to be an easily offended prude to know it. We've all seen examples of young women making poor choices in real life and online, and it's never been easier to make a damaging misstep. The internet is forever, as they say.

Talk to your daughter about the internet and advise her never to put anything online that she wouldn't be proud to have her mother, grandmother, or a future employer see. The same goes for off-line activities. Conservative girls should have a developed sense of propriety, which is largely absent from popular culture today. In a world attempting to redefine prostitution as "sex work" and in which pornography has never been more accessible or less taboo, your daughter won't get this message from her peers. Instead, she'll face a good deal of toxic messaging telling her the opposite.

Parents sometimes struggle to find attire that is both appropriate and fashionable, but it's out there. Far more than just clothes, the way a girl presents herself to the world is a signal of how she views herself. At the Clare Boothe Luce Center, we work with our college interns to help them consider how their attire reflects the seriousness and professionalism they wish to project in the workplace. We sometimes give our young women leaders help shopping for attractive, professional dresses. Teaching your daughter that modesty is a virtue will help protect and bolster her confidence. Our girls are worth so much more than the lies society tells them. They should never disregard their bodies. *Do you not know that your bodies are temples of the Holy Spirit, who is in you, whom you have received from God? You are not your own* (1 Corinthians 6:19). Nor should they discount their privacy or uniqueness in the eyes God. Modesty helps a girl see that her worth is inward, not based on outward appearances.

"Princess Culture" Creates Toads

Well-meaning parents can make the mistake of raising little "princesses" rather than strong, graceful girls. Inculcating faith and a religious outlook in your daughter can help fight against this. Princesses are lovely and darling, but raising a conservative daughter also involves hard work and service. Parents should want their daughters to have ample opportunities and better lives than they had, if possible. But "pedestal parenting" undermines a girl's independence and creates entitlement, which happen to be defining traits of liberalism and government dependency. Free stuff and princess-like adoration might sound nice. It might even feel good to the giver. But it can breed a sense of complacency and entitlement.

Daughters must develop a grateful and appreciative spirit if they don't want to become spoiled brats. This spirit is nurtured and cultivated by faith in God. Faith teaches girls to be thankful for what they have and to work if they want more.

Service is another cornerstone of conservativism, embedded in every major faith—and for good reason. Helping others—especially people in need—eases pain, provides opportunities, and touches lives. It's the right thing to do. But the greatest part about serving others might be how it makes the server feel about herself. Service teaches young women to appreciate what they have and shows them the effect their good deeds can have on others. If you want your daughter to value her worth, sign her up for a service opportunity and let her see what the real world looks like. Appropriate exposure to the outside world will provide context for her blessings. Not every kid grows up in a suburban home with an iPad, air conditioning, and a car. There are poor kids and sick people in every city and town in this country. Service opportunities are limitless, and blessings begin to sink in when girls are appropriately exposed to people who are less fortunate. So, let the "princess" out of the castle. When she sees the real-world hardships others face, she will grow in her appreciation for God's provision and care.

Respecting Elders—Yes, That Means Parents, Too

Teaching your daughter to look towards God will also teach her to respect authority. Honoring your parents, after all, is one of God's commandments. A girl's inner life is rich when she expresses a basic courtesy to others and when she is kind to others. It's also apparent when she demonstrates respect for her elders.

Respect is taught at home. Children learn how to properly relate to authority figures through their relations with their family members and through their faith. When I was raising my own children, my mother was sick for ten years before passing and needed a lot of help every day. The meaningful hours spent helping her taught my children the importance of serving the people they love. Serving their grandmother taught my children that they had obligations that came before themselves. And while they sometimes would have preferred to spend time with their friends, to this day they treasure the bond they formed with their grandmother through serving her.

Respecting others comes first and foremost from respecting your parents and submitting to God. Today, instilling these primary forms of respect for authority is all the more important given our cultural climate. Parents used to exhort their children to respect their teacher, without hesitation. Even if you didn't learn to respect your parents or have faith, you could learn the importance of respect for authority at school.

Parents who want to raise conservative daughters today can't be so trusting. There are left-wing and deviant agendas in education, in both public and private schools. And because the values girls will learn at school may conflict with the values they learn from their parents and from their church, it's essential that young girls be taught whom to respect at home.

Homeschooling is different. Parents have more control over educational influences, and children typically have a lot more interaction with older people. Regardless, girls learn to be more respectful with adults when they have appropriate exposure to them. It's up to parents to determine who those adults are and to adjust expectations of respect accordingly.

The benefits of teaching your daughter to respect her elders last a lifetime. Older adults have life lessons and experiences to share that will not only impact impressionable minds but instill humility and expand horizons. War veterans, Cuban and Vietnamese refugees, Holocaust survivors, civil rights–era Americans, and even the elderly woman next door can help your daughter appreciate the world in a different way. Their contributions and their humanity deserve respect. Some parents ask me whether they should require their daughter to say "yes ma'am" or "yes sir." That's a personal decision often driven by the standard where one lives (in the South the answer is a resounding yes). But thinking about a daughter's tone and language is a good starting point for instilling respect for one's elders.

What if a girl's parents are themselves lacking? Well, bad parents deserve respect too. However, that does not mean daughters have to honor a parent's poor choices. If a father is absent or abusive, then there's absolutely no duty to respect his behavior. Instead, a girl will need an alternate role model. Churches and synagogues are ideal places for girls to find healthy mentors, as many contain married women with successful marriages and careers. When a meaningful relationship is forged with an older woman, it will further foster a girl's respect for her elders.

"Courage Is the Ladder on Which All the Other Virtues Mount"

There will be times when preserving your daughter's self-worth will require her to stand up and fight. She should be encouraged to do so with grace. Conservative girls are not docile, doe-eyed shrinking violets who avoid conflict because they have been taught to turn the other cheek. Nor are they doormats. On the contrary, faith instills a self-worth that strengthens a girl's ability to raise her hand in class and challenge a teacher who's preaching a destructive ideology. There are ways girls can politely point out a teacher's bias. For example, if a teacher is singing the praises of a socialist economist on an issue, she can ask her teacher, "Can you share Nobel Prize–winning economist Milton Freidman's view on that?" Or if a feminist teacher is railing on about how a woman has a right to control her body and have an abortion if she wants, she can ask, "Does science tell us that her baby is part of her body or a separate human being?" Faith also helps girls stand up to boys and peer pressure. It gives them courage.

God means for us to be strong in our beliefs. *For God has not given us a spirit of fear, but of power and of love and of a sound mind* (2 Timothy 1:7). When you come from a place of faith, you are standing up for a righteous cause. You are fighting the good fight, and you're doing something moral. Teach your daughter to have graceful power and that it's possible to have elegance, decorum, and a strong willingness to fight. People of faith believe that we should follow the laws of government until they interfere with God's law. Then, we stand up and speak out.

Girls are often socialized to get along. But when a college professor tells lies or when other students prevent conservative girls from bringing a pro-life speaker to campus, your daughter should know she can and should speak up and be brave. Work with your daughter to give her the tools she needs (more on this later) to be a confident communicator. At the Clare Boothe Luce Center for Conservative Women, we help young conservative women learn how to speak up and fight smart. We teach girls about important policy issues and arm them with key facts to make strong arguments.

That said, you can teach and train until the cows come home, but all of it hinges on courage. Clare Boothe Luce once said, "Courage is the ladder on which all the other virtues mount." Wise words. Luce was saying that you can know everything, you can be the greatest, smartest person in the world, but you have to develop the courage to speak up at the right time and in the right way to oppose people who would diminish you, your family, and your beliefs. And you have to do it gracefully.

Some girls develop courage to speak up and promote conservative ideas very young—in high school or earlier. I was a senior in college before I was brave enough to start a conservative club. It took me a year of living in socialist England (before Margaret Thatcher) in a junior-year exchange program to develop an intense passion for promoting freedom and begin my life's work as a conservative leader.

Luce was graceful and courageous. She had to be. She was the only nationally recognized conservative woman during the first half of the twentieth century other than Margaret Chase Smith. Luce spoke up when no one else would, and she paved the way for other women to follow in her footsteps. She gave speeches. She spoke on the radio. She was an author. She appeared on television when few women, much less conservative women, had the opportunity. Luce had tremendous courage, motivated by her belief in God and her upbringing. Not all of us are called to such a public life, but every girl can develop the courage to defend herself and her conservative beliefs.

If your daughter knows her self-worth flows from God, then she will have the courage to know her voice matters. She'll understand that there's something inside her that's of value and worth defending.

Teach Redemption, because We All Make Mistakes

"Amazing Grace, how sweet the sound..." Those words come from a 250-year-old hymn that was written by John Newton, a former slave trader. As his ship was battered and cast about, nearly sinking during a terrible storm, Newton knelt and prayed. He was sailing human cargo from Africa to the Americas when the storm hit. Amid the crashing waves and the Atlantic abyss below, Newton was moved to return the slaves to their homeland. He later sailed home and became a preacher. Then a hymn writer. The blessed song "Amazing Grace" is his story.

"Amazing grace, how sweet the sound, that saved a wretch like me." One thing that has always stuck with me is that Newton's mother had taken him to church as a child. Saying he strayed from faith would be an understatement. He lived an awful life. But he came back to God, and his testimony of repentance has inspired millions of people over two and a half centuries. So, what is grace? It's the idea that no matter what you've done, you can have a new beginning. What a wonderful and sustaining truth to instill in a young girl's heart.

We all make mistakes. Your daughter will be no different. But if she believes in something bigger than herself, if she has faith, she can always turn the ship around and begin anew. Government cannot restore wounded souls. In the hymn, Newton says, "I once was lost, but now am found,/ Was blind, but now I see." God's forgiveness gives us another chance. Government can't. That's so important for young women to know.

Some young women are angels, but most aren't. I was pretty darn good, but I know I wasn't an angel. If forgiveness and redemption are in your daughter's heart, she can better cope with life's ups and downs. Even when she veers off course—and who among us hasn't—she will know she can turn back and be redeemed. That's grace. And if conservative daughters are to be graceful, then they must know how to receive it.

Faith in Motion

Self-worth is the deep sense of value we have about ourselves. It needs to be nurtured. We have to get in there and fight.

America was built on rules, laws, and morals. They didn't just come from out of the blue. They came from our Judeo-Christian heritage. Most conservatives accept this. Most Americans do too. But these ideas are under attack, and they get twisted by academia, popular culture, and politicians.

Don't let these forces raise your daughter. Take her to church or synagogue. Celebrate meaningful religious ceremonies. Pray together—over meals, trips, tests, decisions, and each other. Talk to her about government and faith. Spend time with family and friends who have faith and understand the limits of government and society. Teach your girl to be courageous. To stand up when her values are under attack. If your daughter never hears about faith, and she never sees anything other than what's in the culture—which often degrades people of faith—she will be adrift when life's hardships come crashing in. When she knows she is wonderfully made, she will know that her self-worth flows from God, not government.

CHAPTER 2

Family First

In November of 1977, 15,000 pro-family supporters changed the course of history. Women from across the country showed up in droves to thwart the government-sponsored National Women's Conference in Houston, Texas. The event was billed as an opportunity for American women to determine the future of our country. The conference was the culmination of a series of regional forums, and abortion and the so-called Equal Rights Amendment (ERA) were on the agenda, as was the government's role in enforcing them. Houston was supposed to be the Left's crowning moment.

But the conference was not really for "all" women as claimed. Conservative pioneer Phyllis Schlafly dubbed it the "Federal Financing of a Foolish Festival for Frustrated Feminists." Schlafly led the pro-family counter-rally, where outnumbered and politically marginalized conservative women championed marriage, homemakers, the sanctity of life, and limited government. "I came here because I felt North Dakota had to be represented at a pro-family rally," a mother of nine told the *New York Times*. Other conservative women expressed similar sentiments. Schlafly herself was a mother of six.

Predictably, these conservative women were pilloried by the press. With smug condescension, they were characterized as opposing women's rights, which was absurd given that they themselves were women. The truth is they had a different vision from the liberal press, one that saw family as a gift rather than a tool of oppression. As a young woman living in Washington, D.C., I had researched the ERA. Like a lot of legislation, it sounded great until you actually looked at it. The pro-family attendees were right: the devil was in the details. Schlafly argued that the ERA would take away women's exemption from the military draft, made unconstitutional single-sex schooling and activities (including sororities, Girl Scouts, and mother-daughter school functions), and removed insurance companies' rights to charge women less than men, amongst other measures to achieve "equality." Ultimately, these conservative women helped defeat the ERA, and with it a massive expansion of government power. This gathering of women began changing the national debate by insisting it was essential that conservative women's views be respected. It was the first time conservative women had organized strictly as mothers, wives, and daughters. ERA was being promoted arrogantly in their name. This gathering showed the country that our women could be galvanized too.

History is filled with courageous conservative women who embraced and defended the traditional family. Many began to have incredible careers promoting conservative ideas outside their homes as well, everyday heroines whom you never hear about. But these women were okay with that. They were too busy putting family first to care who got the credit.

Why Should Family Come First?

Family is where it all begins. Family is the central organizing unit of society, the basic building block of all civilization, especially Western civilization. It's the place where children learn about relationships and rules. When family comes first, children flourish. It's common sense confirmed by decades of studies: intact families are healthier and more prosperous, on average, than broken families.

According to research compiled by the Heritage Foundation, children from traditional families are more likely to find academic success, emotional stability, and good financial outcomes, whereas children raised in single-parent homes are more likely to drop out of school, suffer financial hardship, and commit violent crimes. Indeed, marriage reduces the probability of child poverty by 80 percent.

While girls are less prone to violence and incarceration than boys, family instability increases the odds that they will have relationship difficulties later in life. These heartbreaking "like mother, like daughter" cycles frequently involve a higher incidence of financial distress and single-parent adulthood. But affluence isn't an escape. Daughters of well-to-do divorced parents are more likely to experience depression and anger issues. They also tend to mature faster and take greater social risks.

Let's be clear: there are many legitimate reasons why some children cannot grow up with a mother and a father. And we know government programs have driven fathers from many homes. Indeed, many single moms heroically raise loving children. For me, raising three sons with a husband and with my parents across the street was fulfilling, with many joys, but also very hard. I honestly don't know how these single moms do it. The challenges are many. Lower income single mothers often live in dangerous neighborhoods with all manner of bad influences. These moms want the best for their children just like every parent, and somehow many of these amazing women manage to take their children to church despite working long hours and sometimes multiple jobs. They are truly remarkable. People of faith are called to care for those who need help, and conservatives have an obligation to do the same.

At the same time, it's more than a little ironic that wealthy liberals often choose traditional family lifestyles while pushing damaging anti-family policies on people who can least afford the consequences. Think about it from a practical perspective: four hands raising a daughter and four eyes watching her are better than two. Two paychecks are twice as much as one. In fact, two federal minimum-wage paychecks amount to more than the federal poverty level for a family of four. It's not rocket science; it's simple math. Tack on traditional upward mobility values as opposed to the progressive victim mentality, and poor families have a fighting chance. Immigrant families understand this and in many ways represent the classic American dream.

That said, the traditional family isn't possible for some. Life is messy; things happen outside of one's control. So, what do you do if your family of origin or your marriage is less than ideal? You do the only thing you can—your best. I was recently blessed to have an intern who came from a single-parent family. She was one of the best interns I've ever had. She grew up with her mother, but her grandfather stepped in and helped raise her. Her family is a wonderful testament to the concept of "family first" in its own way. She's an incredible young woman who earned a full scholarship to college.

Extended family relationships often help parents overcome challenges. Forming bonds with aunts and uncles, for example, can greatly enrich your daughter's life. Sometimes grandparents live nearby and can help shoulder the load, as I was blessed to have my parents, who lived right across the street, do. They can't replace a father and mother, but they are loving additions, nonetheless. Growing up with cousins is also wonderful. They often turn into friends who share a family connection. Fostering extended family ties can help a young girl see beyond her own immediate surroundings.

Much to the Left's chagrin, there's overwhelming evidence that the nuclear family is the best framework for individual and societal well-being. It's the cure to so much of what ails us. Yet the family is under constant attack. Radical feminists, post-modern academics, and left wing activist groups have waged war on family and marriage. Why? Because for Leftists, strong families are bad for business. Dependency fuels Leftism. When people have a family they can rely on, they are less likely to rely on government.

Feminists know this. So they discourage the kind of relationships women have with men that make them happy. "A woman needs a man like a fish needs a bicycle," says a feminist credo that encapsulates the Left's thinking. It was first popularized by the feminist icon Gloria

Steinem in the 1960s and has become so common that you can buy T-shirts with this daft slogan on Amazon. Steinem, anointed the "world's most famous feminist," is a lifelong radical who enthusiastically embraces the anti-family activist organization Black Lives Matter.

Consider this broadside that was on the Black Lives Matter website just weeks before the 2020 election: "We disrupt the Western-prescribed nuclear family structure requirement by supporting each other as extended families and 'villages' that collectively care for one another, especially our children, to the degree that mothers, parents, and children are comfortable."

Translation: the Left's goal is to tear down the traditional family.

The Left has a new slogan when it comes to childrearing: "it takes a village to raise a child." Though this sounds relatively harmless, it's in fact a radical proposal that expresses a desire to "disrupt" the traditional family. Students of history might recognize the origin of the unsettling declaration as coming from Marx and Engels's *Communist Manifesto*:

> Abolition of the family!... On what foundation is the present family, the bourgeois family, based? On capital, on private gain. In its completely developed form, this family exists only among the bourgeoisie. But this state of things finds its complement in the practical absence of the family among the proletarians, and in public prostitution.

The Left has declared war on the institution of family precisely because they know and fear its power.

Put another way, marriage is a calling, and family is a gift, that must be protected. Spouses and family members must see each other that way, especially when angry and hurt. We all have good days and bad days, and sometimes we struggle. But we must view the family—both on an individual and a civilizational level—as a wonderful, rich structure that makes all of us better. Some marriages can't be saved. But when they can, the rewards are great for children.

Families are about love. They transcend temporary relationships. You can't change certain things in life, such as where you are born, when you are born, and who your parents are. You get what you get. But when it comes to children, you get what you give. No family is perfect, but putting family first means prioritizing love, encouragement, understanding, hope, comfort, advice, and sacrifice.

Family is the single most important social institution in society. It is also the best defense against poverty, a vehicle for positive relationships, and a source of love and lifelong support. Yet the traditional family is under attack. Radical feminists, left-wing activist groups, and other political pressures are tearing down the family to breed government dependency. More than ever, parents need to put their families first for the good of their daughters and the country.

Marriage is a key aspect of a healthy family, and married parents should prioritize their own relationship over their kids. Supporting and nurturing your spouse models relationship behavior for your daughter while creating family stability. Non-traditional families can also take a "family-first" approach to raising girls by building strong supporting relationships with grandparents, cousins, and church families.

Marriage Comes before Children

Putting your family first can look a lot of different ways. Fundamentally, it's making family a priority. For parents, that means making their relationship primary. Your marriage first, your kids second. This shouldn't be controversial. But in today's youth-obsessed culture, children too often receive a disproportionate share of attention. This creates a two-fold problem: kids grow up with an expectation that the world revolves around them, and marriage relationships suffer.

The love that a mother and father have for each other is the love-model their daughters see. If parents respect and enjoy each other, girls notice. If they fail to nurture their relationship, they are setting a poor example. Parents don't have to take a "children must be seen and not heard" approach, but they do need to establish a healthy relationship structure. And it won't matter what we say if our actions don't match. Children learn by watching, and girls especially need to see their parents in an authentic, loving relationship. They also need to be able to talk about it.

Parents who communicate poorly, or not at all, do their daughters a disservice. Communication is critical. Often spouses who do not talk to each other about what's really going on in their relationship are destined for trouble. Jobs, schedules, and layers of responsibilities that go along with raising kids can make it difficult to invest in a marriage relationship. Husbands and wives need to prioritize their relationship. It's hard; I know. My husband Ron and I have been married half a century. It hasn't been all sparkles and rainbows. In our marriage we operate more as equals. Others prefer the husband to be the clear leader of the family with the wife as his helpmate. Whatever works best for you and makes your marriage successful is what is important. The key is that you and your spouse's North Star—your guiding principle—is that the family comes first. Always.

You might assume that because you are both adults that your needs aren't as important as your children's. Days and weeks may go by without a meaningful conversation. Soon, a husband and wife can start to feel more like roommates than a married couple. Conflict and resentments may get buried for the sake of expediency, but they don't go away. They fester and infect the family. Daughters feel that tension, and they know when something's not right.

It's not about being perfect; we're only human. The question is, how can parents lead their daughter when they are on shaky ground in their own relationship? They're not going to fool teenage girls, that's for sure. So go on dates. Do little favors for your spouse that will be a surprise. Be romantic. Plan something fun, and pray together if you are people of faith. Show your daughter what a real, loving relationship looks like, because that's going to be her model.

When a daughter knows her parents love not only her, but also each other, it gives her a greater sense of security and stability. Children can't help but blame themselves when their parents fight, and even more when they get divorced. When a marriage suffers, kids suffer. No amount of dance classes, volleyball tournaments, or gifts will suffice. Conversely, moms and dads who prioritize their marriage have more credibility when they talk to their daughter about things like dating and marriage. It's easier for your daughter to feel loved when she feels secure, and that means she's less likely to seek validation from those who may not have her best interests in mind.

Couples shouldn't try to *find* time to spend together, they need to *make* time. This can be really hard to do at the end of a long day of work and family life. That's doubly true for working parents, which most parents are these days. Too often, parents devote the bulk of their energy to their careers, and anything left over goes to their kids. Their relationship suffers from a lack of attention. A proactive approach is necessary, because if you don't plan quality time, then it will be spent doing something less important. What would happen if you committed to coming home from work early occasionally, getting a sitter if your kids are young, and going out to dinner with your spouse? I can tell you it will mean a lot to your daughter to see her mom and dad dress up for an evening alone together. It's a simple way to affirm your marriage relationship in front of her.

Backing each other up is another way to show relationship priority. Kids have an uncanny knack for playing one parent off the other in the hopes of getting what they want. Have you ever told your daughter something only for her to turn around and ask your spouse the same question? Showing a united front conveys stability. When parents hold the line, they create stability even if their daughter doesn't like their decision. They are essentially saying, "We're the parents, we love you, and we are making the decision because we are in charge, not you."

Sometimes parents won't agree with each other, and a compromise may be in order. That's normal. But if you argue in front of your daughter, make sure to resolve the dispute in front of her if possible. Or decide, as my husband and I have, that the issue you disagree about probably won't be resolved, and you'll just respectfully live with different views. The last thing she needs is to feel like she has to take sides. A mature conversation followed by forgiveness and amended behavior is a testimony that marriages require work and that families can weather conflict and grow stronger. Putting marriage first isn't just good for parents; it's good for the whole family. Showcasing a healthy relationship model will help your daughter seek the same as she grows older.

Model Conservatism, and Allow Your Daughter to Grow

Putting your daughter's best interests first is also putting family first. Each family member is connected to the whole, and when children do well the team does well. So, when trying to raise a conservative daughter, remember the goal isn't to force her to think a certain way. Nor is it to shower her with praise or show her who's boss. It's to guide her to become the best person she can be while instilling conservative values. Rather than sermonizing constantly on specific policy issues, help your daughter develop self-reliance, kindness, and faith—conservative virtues. Promote her intellectual curiosity and desire to achieve. Model conservative values in your own life, and watch her flourish.

When I was a girl, my parents taught me the classic conservative values of self-reliance and hard work. Sure, I was loved and supported, but I was expected to work and solve my own problems in protected areas, like school. I learned that hard work was rewarded in life and that entitlement wasn't an option. Every morning before my siblings and I would leave the house for school, my father would exhort us to "get in there and fight." That's what Dad said, and that's what he did. He went to work, to the Naval Reserve, and to NYU at night, earning a master's degree and working on a Ph.D., while providing for our family. And my mother, such a warm and giving person from the generation when almost all mothers were stay-at-home moms, kept everything at home running smoothly while he was gone. Dad never said, "Go out there and be careful," or, "Call me and I'll take care of it." He taught me that life is a looming battle waiting to be fought, so you have to get in there and make a difference. My parents made me figure it out, because that was in my best interest. That's the same approach we have used at the Clare Boothe Luce Center to mentor thousands of conservative young women.

Putting family first also means learning to let go and send your daughter into the world at some point. It's not easy, and there are risks, but she's going to have to learn to solve her own problems. Parents can certainly help, but when mom and dad hover and take care of everything they are not allowing their girl to grow. Many parents make this mistake without realizing it. They love their daughter so much that they will do anything to make her happy. But that's a recipe for dependence and panic. Girls who haven't had a chance to mature often run into trouble when they leave home. Their happiness and security are affected when they don't know how to deal with bumps in the road. Sometimes they become anxious and depressed while away at school. Sometimes they misbehave. An inability to cope with stressful situations can also lead to health problems, such as eating disorders or self-medicating.

Start with the approach that you can never be too loving. You are not going to spoil your daughter by loving her too much. That only happens when you give her things in place of love. Real love is unconditional, and there's an endless supply. But that doesn't mean giving your daughter constant adoration and unearned praise. And it doesn't mean setting such low expectations that she can't fail. When necessary, love can look like discipline, and it should be "tough" when it's in her best interest.

Every child has moments when she resists what she needs to do. Don't let your daughter off the hook. Help her navigate challenges without solving them for her. If she fails, or if she messes up, don't always bail her out. That only invites more problems and a dependency or preference for others to fix her mistakes. Instead, walk her through the process of learning from a mistake. Teach her that blaming others and making excuses won't cut it. Neither will perfectionism. Many girls grow up eager to please and are terrified to make a bad grade or fall out of favor with their peers. It's understandable. But playing it safe doesn't allow for growth, and conservative women need to take healthy risks in life to effect change. Parents can help instill the confidence to risk failure by nurturing a foundation of unconditional love and the habit of facing life's challenges head on.

It's also critical that you recognize your daughter's uniqueness. What works for another child may not be the best for her. Be willing to adjust and understand that growth can sometimes look like rebelliousness. The same quality that makes your daughter argumentative at home may be what makes her a courageous debate champ at school. So, be prepared to grow with her.

Establishing general ground rules helps your girl know where she stands. It's also helpful to identify and communicate non-negotiable behaviors for when disputes arise. Sometimes parents will have to pull rank, but putting your daughter's interests first and consistently taking the time to explain your decisions as much as possible is key. It may be more work to hash out your thinking, but it builds trust.

Safety

Early years are a time of innocence, and it's incumbent on parents to protect their daughters as a first order of family business. Threats aren't just physical. Parents need to protect their daughters from damaging cultural influences and corrosive social media. Never in history have girls been more exposed to immoralism of all forms. Unfortunately, school is another area where parents must be more involved. When I grew up, parents mostly shared the same values. We didn't have K-12 political controversies, anti-American curricula, or boys in the girls' bathroom. But Leftist agendas now pop up as early as elementary school.

Did you know that many school systems teach twelve years of compulsory sexual education disguised as something called "Family Life"? I live in Fairfax County, Virginia, a suburb of Washington, D.C., and our schools, both public and private, are considered high-performing. But some of the things they teach children are totally inappropriate, like the multi-year sex-ed program that was forced on my middle child. There was definitely a weirdo agenda behind it, and some of the content was just bizarre. We objected, and the school made it difficult for us to opt out. They sent my child to the library instead to complete large research projects. And that was in the fifth grade. Kids who didn't participate were made to feel stigmatized. We pulled him out of our neighborhood government-run school shortly thereafter.

It was an ordeal that saddened us. But we believed that protecting our child's moral formation was important. The point is that parents have to know what's going on in their children's schools. You can't allow politically driven administrators to have free rein over your daughter. There was a time when you could trust teachers and administrators. Not anymore. We recently had a local school board vote where eleven of twelve board members voted to allow boys into girls' bathrooms. Only one member raised her hand to dissent from such an obviously bad decision. If these policies are proliferating around the nation's capital, they will almost certainly arrive in your city or town, if they haven't already.

If your daughter is in school—whether public or private—get involved. You don't have to run for PTO president, but you need to see what's going on. What types of values are being taught? What is she learning? Are they teaching the revisionist, anti-American 1619 Project, or is 1776 or 1789 the year of America's founding? Boys will often come home and mock their teachers. You'll know exactly what's off in their classrooms. But girls may not be so forthcoming. In my experience, girls more often want to protect their parents from controversy.

One approach is to work both ends, the school and your daughter. Communicate with her teachers, and instill the idea that things will be better for her if she's open and honest about what's going on in the classroom because you'll know about it anyway. Build an early firewall. Show her she's protected. Teach her that your family may not always look or act like other families—and that's a good thing.

That certainly applies to social media. Honesty is the best policy when it comes to social media. Most parents still don't understand how powerful it is. Facebook, Instagram, Twitter, Snapchat, TikTok, and other global platforms are immensely influential, and they are here to stay. Kids today have never known a world without the internet, and banning access to it is not realistic. Children as young as five and six years old are now given smartphones and iPads. Older kids are quite savvy about their internet use.

Statistics show that parents largely fail to restrict harmful content. Hardcore pornography and other damaging subject matter have never been more accessible. But another widespread harm for girls is that social media allows users to create virtual personalities, which can undermine your daughter's confidence in who she is. Fake lives are curated to show flawless beauty and extravagant materialism. When it's not pitting us against each other, social media sells an idealized version of life that is not reality. Many girls I've worked with say there's a temptation to compete for "likes." They are motivated to seek virtual validation. When they don't get it, they feel they are doing something wrong in their real lives, that they are somehow less than the girls on the screen. But it's not true. It's all a filtered, algorithmic illusion. The solution? Get back to basics.

Instead of allowing their daughters to spend hours online every day, conservative parents need to impose limits. Restricting access to harmful websites and curtailing general screen time is a good place to start. When my children were growing up, cell phones were not yet widespread. If I were raising them now, I would delay giving them a cell phone as long as possible, even though "all the other kids" have one. Never allow technology to distract from family time. And above all, encourage your daughter to develop in ways that far surpass social media approval. Why should she settle for an empty online life when she can spend time with family and friends and enrich her real life? Encourage your daughter to look at the real world more than she stares at a screen. Teach her to join a church youth group and support fulfilling pursuits, like music, art, and sports. Let her see you reading good books, so she does too. Some great books I highly recommend include: *Anne of Green Gables* by Lucy

Montgomery, *Little Women* by Louisa May Alcott, *Jane Eyre* by Charlotte Brontë, *The Diary of Anne Frank*, *The Lion, the Witch and the Wardrobe* series by C. S. Lewis, *Pride and Prejudice* and all the books by Jane Austen, *An American Life: The Autobiography* by Ronald Reagan, *A Tree Grows in Brooklyn* by Betty Smith, and *A Christmas Carol* by Charles Dickens. This lists just a few; there are so many wonderful books and good stories for her. Give your daughter healthy alternatives to the shallow and phony world of social media, and she won't be dependent on it. Instead, she'll see right through it.

Balance Is the Key to Family and Career

An essential element to raising a conservative daughter is for parents to make sure that they themselves raise their children, not government, not school, and not pop culture. That's what it means to put family first. But how can parents do this in an age when careers take priority over family? Breadwinners often work long hours to provide for their loved ones. Unfortunately, that can do more harm than good if they are rarely home or too tired to cherish their daughters when they are. It's not just a breadwinner problem, either. According to Pew Research, nearly half of all parents in two-parent households work full-time jobs, and 72 percent of moms work full or part time jobs. The obvious benefit is two paychecks, but at what cost?

Family suffers when careers are always put first. Building a career is exciting, and a mother or father may be passionate about his or her work. But your daughter needs you. She needs your time and for you to be present during shared time. The key is being present mentally and emotionally to create quality time with her. That's why balance is so important. When she wants to talk, shut off your phone and close your laptop. I know this can be really hard to do with the kinds of jobs so many of us have today, but it is important. It shows her she's a priority.

Working parents can have both a loving family and a successful career if they are willing to plan and sacrifice. I worked for twelve consecutive years in the Reagan and George H. W. Bush administrations with children. I then founded the Clare Boothe Luce Policy Institute, now known as the Clare Boothe Luce Center for Conservative Women. My husband has had a successful career as well. From the beginning, we prioritized our marriage and children, but our jobs promoting conservatism were important to our family and our country. It wasn't easy or perfect, and we made our share of mistakes. But our commitment to our family acted as a guiding principle.

Most married women and mothers work today, so there is a constant balancing act between work-life and home-life. There are some benefits to this arrangement, especially for daughters. Children grow up seeing what work looks like. A strong work ethic helps a girl realize that one day she can also have a family and a career if she chooses. Girls need to see possibilities. They need to learn that you have to work hard no matter what you choose to do. You study hard in school, you work in your relationships, and you work to make yourself the kind of person you want to be.

It's tempting to cut corners even when you dedicate yourself to your family. Just remember, you won't get the time back. While you are spending extra time at the office, she is looking for someone else to help with her science project. You won't get a second chance to teach her how to ride a bike or go fishing. And she will remember the love you showed her by your presence for the rest of her life.

Plan family events and guard them jealously. The great U.S. Supreme Court justice Antonin Scalia famously made it home for dinner every night during the work week. Scalia and his wife Maureen raised nine children and had thirty grandchildren. He admonished his clerks to always "be home for dinner" and claimed that "children are civilized at the dinner table." Consider grounding your "family-first" commitment on the dinner table. Make it a goal, and build on it. You may be surprised how quickly the simple, consistent act of breaking bread with your daughter can enrich your relationship. Where better to express your conservative perspective with her? Where better for her to learn from you? Many of our children's friends scoffed at them for having to "be home for dinner" every night. But that family time was so important through the years, and now they are grown and come to our home every Sunday for dinner with their children—one of our life's best highlights.

President Reagan put it best in his farewell address to the nation: "Let me offer lesson number one about America: all great change in America begins at the dinner table. So, tomorrow night in the kitchen, I hope the talking begins. And children, if your parents haven't been teaching you what it means to be an American, let 'em know and nail 'em on it. That would be a very American thing to do."

Give and Ye Shall Receive

A major flaw in Leftist ideology and feminism is that they are selfish mindsets. It's a "me-first" outlook. "Family first" is about giving. The happiest women I know prioritize their families and give the most. They elevate their loved ones by serving them, and in return receive the blessings and joy that come through giving. Unfortunately, that concept is lost on women who believe that marriage and children hold them back—or worse, that it's a tool of patriarchal oppression. They end up missing out on so much that life has to offer.

I'm constantly amazed at how women's activist groups push selfish pathologies. The love-your-body campaigns, for example, go out of their way to embrace unhealthy lifestyles. Being proud of who you are and how you look is a good thing, except when your health is at risk. If your daughter struggles with her weight, encouraging fitness is deemed fat-shaming by some. But "family first" doesn't indulge poor choices. It uplifts loved ones and says, "I love you, and I will give you everything I can to support your well-being."

A giving mindset is tied to faith, and it involves sacrifice. Some call it the "I'm-third" approach: trust in God, give to others, then pursue your desires. The mystery of giving is that you receive more than what you give, but that's not why we do it. We give because we love and because it's the right thing to do. And I know that the happiest and most content people in my life, like my mother and mother-in-law, were the biggest givers I ever knew. The biggest takers I've known, meanwhile, were not so happy and content.

Family service often starts with communication. How you talk to your daughter is every bit as important as what you want to say. That applies to spouses, too. Being thoughtful helps address underlying problems, and kindness builds trust while maintaining a firm stance. Subtle differences in verbal and nonverbal communication also make a big impact. If you need to talk to your daughter about something serious, be compassionate and open-minded. Don't assume that you know what she's going through because you were once her age. Ask open-ended questions to spark conversation, such as: "What was the best part of your day? What is your biggest dream? If you could tell or ask me anything, without condemnation, what would you say? How are your friends doing? What's your favorite tradition our family has? If we could hop on an airplane today to go anywhere in the world, where would you want to go?" Then listen and look for ways to support her.

Wealthy parents sometimes write their daughters a check instead of spending time with them, but no amount of money can buy love or reclaim lost time. Families need to have dinner together, sit together, tell stories, laugh, and talk things through. They need traditions. Whether it's Christmas, Hanukkah, Thanksgiving, Independence Day, or an annual vacation, family traditions keep the spirit of giving alive. They also give a girl something fun and meaningful to look forward to.

Giving can look many different ways, but ultimately it is about love. Yes, one can give too much, and that's something to consider. But when an "I'm third" approach is taken, marriage and parent-child relationships are infused with grace. Giving creates loyalty and closeness. It means not judging a loved one too harshly when he or she makes a mistake; rather, it involves serving that person's needs. When your daughter makes a mistake, give her the gift of forgiveness and consequences. Emphasize her strengths, share your experiences, and stay connected with her even when she pushes you away. What bounces back may surprise you.

CHAPTER 3

America Is Exceptional and Worth Defending

We are so blessed to live in the United States of America. Never in history has there been a freer, more prosperous, and more powerful place than the one we call home. Think about that. By what miracle did we receive such an inheritance? The answer is in every way tied to our founding principles and the sacrifices of innumerable patriots, past and present. When parents impress this upon their daughters, gratitude and pride are sure to follow. Reverence for the flag, respect for the uniform, and a desire to defend freedom become natural impulses, born from loving this great land.

Our Founders certainly believed that. And many gave their lives for those beliefs. Chief among these ideals was the solemn belief that our rights are God-given, not given to us from government. No other country in the history of the world was created on this concept. The Founders understood this and made America exceptional among the nations of the world—a country where freedom and virtue could produce a nation of unrivaled prosperity and goodwill.

Unfortunately, however, not everyone chooses to see the good in our country. Many colleges and mass media outlets are determined to portray America in the worst possible light. It's unconscionable. Leftist propaganda makes it difficult for girls to understand our unique nature, making it all the more important for parents to be a guiding light. The *New York Times*, for example, has embraced the radical 1619 Project, which claims our nation was not founded in 1776, but in 1619, when slaves were first brought to North America. The project asserts that the Revolutionary War was waged to defend slavery, not to overthrow an abusive monarchy. Despite gross inaccuracies, the liberal revisionist campaign is now taught in public schools.

Professional athletes kneel during the national anthem, protesting a nation that affords them the opportunity to make millions for playing a game. If anything, these athletes are soaked in the wonders of American capitalism, but radical activist groups have morphed them into political activists who prefer to denigrate our country rather than celebrate it. Football stars like Colin Kaepernick and U.S. Women's National Soccer team player Megan Rapinoe have even monetized anti-Americanism, while corporate patrons like Nike rake in billions of dollars from "woke" endorsement revenues. It's a cynical exploitation that leaves many children with a false impression about their rights and opportunities. It's not fair to them. But it's not hopeless, either.

If there is one thing I have learned that's worth repeating, it's that parents cannot rely on government and culture to raise their daughter. The good news is that there are many ways for parents to teach girls to appreciate our exceptional country, flaws and all, and conserve the blessings that were bought and paid for by previous generations. Many paid the ultimate price. And there is no shortage of brave men and women who currently dedicate themselves to securing peace for the rest of us. We should be so grateful!

As you set about instilling patriotism in your daughter, remember that the stakes are high. As conservative African American sports journalist Jason Whitlock said during a Hillsdale College lecture, "A country that no longer believes in its founding ideals cannot prosper and survive." On that account, I'd like to pose a question: If your daughter asked you about our founding ideals, what would you say?

Know Your History

It's my experience that many students lack a clear understanding of our national origin. It's not their fault. Even well-raised, conservative college girls struggle to articulate the ideals that make our country special. The Constitution, unprecedented wealth, and maybe the military, is what they point to when asked. When parents know history and how to explain it during dinner table–type discussions, they can combat misinformation and provide a positive description of where we come from and where we need to go.

American Exceptionalism means that America is special and unique because we acknowledge that God, not government, gives us our rights. Government's job is to protect those God-given rights. It's a recognition that our country is unique. Most nations are built on the basis of a common ethnicity, history, culture, national religion, or ruling family. The United States, however, stands alone in that it was built on an idea. America was founded on this idea of God-given rights. Most governments tell their people what they can do. Under our Constitution, "We the People" tell the government it must protect our rights.

The Declaration of Independence states:

> When in the course of human events, it becomes necessary for one people to dissolve the political bands which have connected them with another, and to assume among the powers of the earth, the separate and equal station to which the Laws of Nature and of Nature's God entitle them, a decent respect to the opinions of mankind requires that they should declare the causes which impel them to the separation.
>
> We hold these truths to be self-evident, that all men are created equal, that they are endowed by their Creator with certain unalienable Rights, that among these are Life, Liberty and the pursuit of Happiness....

This is a powerful concept with profound implications, and it is the foundation for the liberties and prosperity we enjoy today. This is what makes us the "Shining city on the Hill." No other country in the history of the world was created out of this concept that our Founding Fathers emphatically relied on; namely, that our rights are God-given, not given to us by government. It's important for parents to discuss our founding with their daughters and take extra steps to bring our unique history to life. One way to do this is to take a trip to Washington, D.C. The National Archives Museum, for example, houses the founding documents that spell out our God-given rights, including the Declaration of Independence, the U.S. Constitution, and the Bill of Rights, and they are open for public viewing.

Visiting the nation's capital is both an experience and education for children. Academic textbooks and abstract conversations can't hold a candle to standing on the steps of the Jefferson and Lincoln Memorials, visiting the World War II Memorial, or looking up at the great Washington Monument. Teach your children that George Washington refused to serve more than two terms and had faith in people, not government. The White House, the Capitol building, and the Supreme Court are magnificent treasures for young minds that teach them about limiting government. Unfortunately, many of the great D.C. museums are run by the Left and are used to promote their big-government philosophy. For example, the National Portrait Gallery exhibits show how great liberal President LBJ was, while stressing that President Reagan ignored AIDS.

When daughters learn through personal experience, they are more likely to feel attached to what they are learning about and have lasting memories. A Washington, D.C., trip could help your daughter learn more about America, what makes it exceptional, and why it is so critical to defend. She may also acquire a sense of context for recent history and current events. School children today might not be overly familiar with President Ronald Reagan, for example, but when they learn about the founding, they will better understand why he took up the mantle of American Exceptionalism in the face of the Soviet Union.

President Reagan saw the dangers of allowing the Left to chip away at our national memory through revisionist history. "Are we doing a good enough job teaching our children what America is and what she represents in the long history of the world?" he asked rhetorically. "We've got to do a better job of getting across that America is freedom—freedom of speech, freedom of religion, freedom of enterprise. And freedom is special and rare. It's fragile; it needs protection." Reagan also encouraged parents to know and teach their children accurate American history. "We've got to teach history based not on what's in fashion but what's important—why the Pilgrims came here, who Jimmy Doolittle was, and what those thirty seconds over Tokyo meant." How many girls know these facts of history and others? The only way our girls will know is if we teach them.

Your daughter may be swayed by cheap rhetorical attacks on our country and the desecration of historic monuments by left-wing mobs. The radical Leftists who clamor for socialist revolution in the streets and to destroy our Constitution twist and distort U.S. history. We didn't always live up to American Exceptionalism, but the Left is determined to erase and replace American history with lies. As Milan Kundera famously wrote, "The first step in liquidating a people is to erase its memory. Destroy its books, its culture, its history. Then have someone write new books, manufacture a new culture, invent a new history. Before long the nation will begin to forget what it is and what it was." Chilling words that demonstrate why we must teach our daughters real history.

"Thank You for Your Service"

It's remarkable to think how small a percentage of the population protects the rest of us. Men and women across America volunteer to put themselves in harm's way to keep the rest of us safe. Most people don't even think about the sacrifices of military servicemen and women as they go about their daily lives. While civilians are at the gym, the office, or relaxing on the couch, brave souls stand guard in faraway lands and across the world's oceans to make sure there is peace at home and that our allies are protected abroad.

It will be easy for your daughter to grow up taking the sacrifices these men make for granted. Unless, of course, you take the time to point out the many ways her life is markedly better off because strong warriors stand ready to defend her freedoms.

There are lots of ways you can help your daughter connect the dots between her life and the sacrifices military volunteers make. For example, those trips abroad that your daughter can't wait to explore and enjoy—those are made possible by the American forces who make the world safe for them. Men and women who serve in hostile locations far from their families sacrifice so much of normal everyday life that we take for granted. Impress that upon your daughter—and that her rights and ability to travel worldwide or work for a company that sells products overseas is made possible because of our armed forces.

Help your daughter to see that national security directly impacts her life. The horrific case of *Wall Street Journal* writer Daniel Pearl, who was kidnapped and beheaded by terrorists in Pakistan, is a haunting reminder that military and intelligence officers protect Americans from gruesome violence when they travel abroad. The September 11 attacks, while rare instances of terrorism on U.S. soil, should remind her that strong military and intelligence services allow us to be safe here in the United States. When President Reagan directed U.S. armed forces to invade Grenada and rescue American students, the mission was only successful because we had a strong military to complete it. And as your daughter sees how her freedoms are inextricably bound to the sacrifices our troops make, her heart will naturally desire to show appreciation.

An easy way to give back is to thank a military member, especially when you are with your daughter. Whether an active duty soldier, sailor, airman, or Marine, a simple "thank you for your service" helps them feel appreciated. Older veterans respond particularly well to children respectfully approaching them to offer gratitude. Parents can also help their daughters make care packages for troops serving overseas. There are many local and national organizations that facilitate mailing them, and care packages with thank-you cards make great activities that girls of all ages can participate in.

If you know any military families in your community, consider helping them. They could certainly use it. Combat soldier salaries certainly don't match the sacrifices our troops make. Moreover, long deployments mean time away from spouses and children. If a mother or father is deployed, your daughter could provide a nice meal, do some yardwork, or help with babysitting needs. Visiting an elder veteran in a retirement home is another wonderful way to show respect for the military and care for those who have worn the uniform. Girls get so much out of serving others, and older adults thrive on youthful interactions. Listening to a senior veteran share about his or her experiences is also an educational opportunity unlike anything your daughter is likely to find on television or social media. These activities connect generations and disparate walks of life, which is critical to nurturing the social bonds that hold our country together.

Parents also need to arm their daughters with knowledge. It's bad enough for service members and war veterans to feel taken for granted, but there is a potent anti-war Left that treats the military as if it's evil. Conservatives know this isn't true. Girls with veteran and active-duty relatives understand that the U.S. armed forces are overwhelmingly a force for good. It's so easy to criticize the military, especially when there's no cost involved. Some of the most vicious attacks come from the ivory towers of academia and liberal student-activist groups who enjoy the freedoms to travel and trade secured by the very people they disparage.

Girls should know that the world is full of conflicts that require difficult choices. And when America acts, it does so to protect its people or liberate others. When the United States dropped atomic bombs on the Japanese cities of Hiroshima and Nagasaki, our military caused unspeakable levels of destruction. But it also saved millions of lives, including that of my father. He was on a U.S. Navy aviation fuel ship in the Pacific during World War II. The atom bomb likely saved his life. Our participation in World War II not only crushed Imperial Japan and ended Nazi Germany, it liberated Jews. Without U.S. military might, how would the Holocaust, the greatest crime in history committed against a single people, have been stopped?

U.S. taxpayers funded the rebuilding of Western Europe and Japan after World War II rather than claiming them as spoils of war. Today, Germany and Japan are free societies and economic powerhouses. The same goes for Korea. American military intervention led to a free and prosperous South, while Communist North Korea remains a totalitarian nightmare. U.S. forces also came home after bitter fighting in Vietnam, and a minimal troop presence remains in Iraq and Afghanistan, mostly to provide security for those living in fear of violence.

What's extraordinary about America is that despite amassing the most powerful military and economic engine ever known, we do not indiscriminately invade and annex foreign lands, even though that is the historic norm. Instead, we gave precious human and material resources to make the world a safer, more prosperous place. Parents can drive this home by visiting war memorials, battlefields, and sights that honor our troops. There is no way to visit Arlington National Cemetery, for example, without realizing that freedom isn't free—it comes through those willing to give the "last full measure of devotion." The next time your daughter sees a young man or woman in uniform at an airport, or an elderly gentleman wearing a veteran's hat at the grocery store, she will be much more inclined to honor their sacrifice.

First Responders Are Heroes

On September 11, 2001, our nation suffered the worst attack on American soil since Pearl Harbor sixty years earlier. But rather than targeting a naval base, passenger jets were hijacked and rammed into giant office buildings in downtown Manhattan. The depravity of such an act, along with the simultaneous attack at the Pentagon and downed airliner in rural Pennsylvania, is beyond comprehension. I remember vividly the loss of Barbara Olson on 9/11, who was scheduled to speak at an event for the Luce Center just a few days later. Never forget that while thousands of civilians scurried for safety, first responders sprang into action.

First responders run toward emergencies so the rest of us can run from them. At the World Trade Center, police officers and firefighters raced into the burning buildings to rescue anyone they could find. Of the nearly 3,000 fatalities that day, 412 were emergency workers, including firefighters from 75 different New York City stations. These were moms and dads who had clocked into work that morning and never came home. That's why Young America's Foundation helps students of all ages, including many of the young women we work with on other projects, host a 9/11 Never Forget Project event on campus, complete with three thousand American flags to honor the lives of each person slaughtered at the hands of radical Islamic terrorists. Visit www.yaf.org/events/911-never-forget-project to get your girl her own step-by-step guide on how to plan and organize an event.

Of course, the tragedy of a fallen first responder is a near daily occurrence in America. Yet the law enforcement community is now vilified in the streets and in the media. Statistics and facts prove they do not deserve such ill treatment, but rare instances of wrongdoing are amplified for ideological ends. In her book *The War on Cops*, criminal justice scholar and Luce Center speaker Heather Mac Donald warns that the conservative idea of respecting law and order is no longer the mainstream viewpoint. During a Clare Boothe Luce Center women's lecture series, Mac Donald explained that widespread protests and attacks on police in recent years are putting lives at risk. The Left's "Defund the Police" movement is an abhorrent, if predictable, result of such vilification.

Parents can help their daughters stand up for law and order and avoid the vicious smears that now permeate left-leaning circles by teaching them to respect the law and those whose job it is to enforce it. Ask your daughter: If someone stole the family car, threatened her with violence, or broke into your house in the middle of the night, what would she do?

Let her think it through. At some point she will probably say, "Call the police." Explain what that entails. When something goes wrong, you dial a phone number, and courageous men and women arrive. They are ready to put themselves in harm's way to defend you. What would we do without them? Keep in mind that many officers have families, yet they take terrible risks to protect innocent strangers every day. They are not the bad guys.

There are many ways to show appreciation for law enforcement officers. Parents can attend a "Back the Blue" event with their daughter, or even host. These are wonderful opportunities to support the police at a time when they are under attack. Your daughter will also see them as the regular people that they are. Police officers are moms, dads, husbands, and wives who chose a noble and dangerous career path for modest pay. Some people are accountants, doctors, and lawyers, and some carry a badge and a gun to protect and serve their community.

Your daughter will naturally come to admire law enforcement when she sees that the vast majority of officers are good people, not the caricatures liberals make them out to be online and in partisan news. Your daughter will also realize that good cops are often put in impossible situations and that they generally have no tolerance for bad apples within their ranks.

Parents can further coordinate a police meet-and-greet with their daughter's school or extracurricular activity groups. They can help raise money for fallen officer funds, have their daughter write a letter of appreciation to a local newspaper, purchase a law enforcement officer's coffee at a local coffee shop, or write a thank-you note to a policeman or sheriff's deputy in your family or neighborhood. Small acts drive home the lesson.

The same goes for firefighters. School events, fundraising, heartwarming letters of thanks, and homemade meals given to your local station with a smile go an awfully long way. Firefighters need our support. The majority of firefighters in America are volunteers. That means they show up to an emergency without making a penny. Volunteers and public employees alike also commonly lack tools and disposable medical equipment and spend their own money to buy what they need. Consider checking in with your local fire crew to see if you and your daughter can help.

But short of that, thank a police officer or firefighter when you are with your daughter. And if you ever receive emergency help, make sure to follow up with the responders involved. Trust me, it means a lot. So much about raising a conservative daughter is about teaching respect for those who sacrifice.

Fight for the American Dream

The American Dream is alive and well, and your daughter should ignore anyone who tells her otherwise. Hard work and upward mobility are hallmarks of traditional America, and people come from all over the world for a chance to earn a better life. If identity politics is to be believed, these people should turn around and run the other way. Try as they may, liberals who wish to disparage our country cannot square the reality that millions upon millions of people work their way to prosperity or come here to experience the land of opportunity.

The Left likes to say that the reason America is "exceptional" (if they'll even concede as much) is because of our economic success. In other words, were it not for our wealth, we'd be just another land mass occupied by ordinary people. This is, of course, absurd. For one, many of our Founding Fathers were poor. There were no colleges, no libraries, no world-class health care facilities at the time of our founding. Moreover, our Founding Fathers left other countries that had better economies and services in order to come to America. And why did they do that? Because they longed for a new—indeed, exceptional—form of limited government that recognized that individual rights flow from God, not rulers.

This should be a source of great pride for your daughter. Teach her that freedom and opportunity are magnets for humanity. Young people are indoctrinated with the opposite message in schools and media, and it's a huge problem. According to Gallup, four in ten Americans now embrace some form of socialism. Put another way, they reject the American Dream.

Perhaps they think that government control of the economy would magically wipe out student loans and health care premiums. But at what cost? High taxes, fewer jobs, imperiled small businesses? Conservatives know that there won't be enough money to deliver on all those "free" promises. There never is. As Margaret Thatcher once said, "The problem with socialism is that you eventually run out of other people's money." And that's only half the trouble. Antifa radicals, Black Lives Matter activists, and many others want a full-scale overthrow of America's economic system—where you work hard, keep your nose clean, and improve the lives of your children and grandchildren. The fastest way to equality, they believe, is to take someone else's earnings, to tear down the system and replace it with politically engineered outcomes. That's why our girls must know and be taught the truth.

You can help prepare your daughter to debate these ideas with her peers. Keep in mind that numbers and spreadsheets aren't as effective as learning first principles. Conservatives often lose when they make good-faith accounting arguments. Saying "we can't afford it" might be true, but it isn't persuasive to someone who is emotionally conditioned with bad information. A better way is for your daughter to appeal to morality: "How can you embrace socialism when it crushes the human spirit? Where has it worked? The American Dream sets people free by rewarding effort and creativity. There will always be wealth inequality, but freedom raises the quality of life for all."

Socialism is based on envying and coveting—teach your daughters not to envy and covet. Teach them to avoid the seven deadly sins that give rise to other bad behaviors—pride, greed, wrath, envy, lust, gluttony, and sloth.

The naysayers' real disagreement is with capitalism, or as the Founders might have called it, industriousness. Free markets make for free people because they allow individuals to pursue life, liberty, and the pursuit of happiness, or property, better than any other economic system. That's why entrepreneurship and innovation are largely an American phenomenon, and oppressive societies like China copy and steal what we produce.

In America, you are free to disagree. If you don't like what's offered, you don't have buy it. There are many choices. With socialism, people will have very little, if any, choice. Look at Venezuela, a country that has the world's *largest* oil reserves, for example. Socialism has turned an oil-rich country into a basket-case tyranny that is unable to provide baby food and toilet paper to its people. Teach your daughter the moral case for capitalism, and that hard work and competition produce opportunity and freedom.

Amending Our Flaws, Embracing the Future

America isn't perfect; it never will be. But that is no reason to ignore the good in our country or erase our past. Show your daughter that it's healthy to face our national flaws and be proud of the progress that we have made.

One of the most disturbing trends in recent memory is the tearing down of historic statues. In both large cities and small towns, left-wing mobs have taken to the streets to exact retribution against symbols of American history. First, they swarmed Confederate statues, citing anti-slavery as their cause. There are legislative processes to remove and replace these types of monuments in every state, but violent crowds overwhelmed police, and weak elected leaders emboldened them by standing down.

Predictably, the mobs didn't stop at Civil War relics. Statues of George Washington, Abraham Lincoln, Christopher Columbus, and even abolitionists like Matthias Baldwin have been defaced and destroyed. Courthouses and federal buildings came next. It's so disheartening, and conservatives are rightly appalled. But parents can counter these dangerous events by turning their attention to their daughter and teaching her that while slavery is part of our past and a terrible stain on our nation, it's also true that no other country has done more to end it. More than 600,000 American lives were given up to end slavery in America.

This is another area where knowing your history is crucial. Like all of us, the Founders were a product of their time, and they built the United States in a way that put slavery on the path to "ultimate extinction," as Abraham Lincoln explained during the Lincoln–Douglas debates. Twenty years after the Constitution was ratified, Congress banned the importation of slaves, but failed to abolish slavery itself, even though slavery was prohibited by the 1787 Northwest Ordinance. By 1860, fifteen states still allowed the abominable practice, and the nation could proceed no further. The Civil War erupted and ripped through the country, killing more Americans than all other wars combined at a time when the country was one tenth its current population.

American Exceptionalism has never been about one group of people or another, but a special principle available to all. Slavery was a denial of those principles, and it was fated to end because it was evil. Unfortunately, such topics have become so forbidden that many girls are afraid to talk about them, even when they know what they are being taught is wrong. So parents cannot be afraid to teach the truth.

What's unique about America is not that we had slavery, like many places in the world, but that we fought a war against ourselves to end it. Parts of the Middle East and Africa still have slavery today, and the Western Hemisphere had slavery long before the first Europeans arrived, including among the American Indians, Aztecs, and Mayans. America is imperfect, but not irredeemable. We have struggled mightily at times, but no other country has done more to realize such ambitious ideals. Help your daughter become a student of history. Visit Civil War battlefields and museums, research historical moments together, discuss uncomfortable subjects, and give her permission to stand up for America regardless of what liberals say. As for great American history books that teach real history, consider the following: *A Patriot's History of the United States* by Larry Schweikart and Michael Allen; *The Myth of the Robber Barons* by Burt Folsom; *Harriet Tubman* by Ann Petry; *Vindicating the Founders* by Thomas West; *Lydia Bailey* by Kenneth Roberts; and *My Ántonia* by Willa Cather. Read these and others like them with your daughter. You'll be glad you did.

Get Going

There is so much to love about America, and there's so much to be thankful for. But freedom, as they say, isn't free. Conserving it for the next generation requires parents to get engaged with the people, places, and ideas that make America great. The more you involve your daughter, the more hope there will be that our blessings of liberty and prosperity will continue.

Parents can begin today by not letting an opportunity pass to thank a veteran or first responder when they are with their daughter. Talk about why it's important to respect men and women who sacrifice to keep us safe. But don't let those conversations become abstract. Attend a "Back the Blue" event, raise money for families of fallen military members, and make a homecooked meal for your local firehouse. Plan a family trip to Washington, D.C., and visit the Freedom Tower, built to replace the World Trade Center, in downtown Manhattan. There is no shortage of ways to learn and give back.

Teach your daughter to take service and sacrifice seriously, and to take pride in expressing her patriotism. Parades, Independence Day celebrations, and other such fruits of the American Dream can make for positive, formative experiences that help girls feel good about who they are and where they are from. There is plenty of negativity from the country's detractors. But it doesn't have to dictate your daughter's point of view. She will win by standing tall, working hard, and honoring all that makes America exceptional.

CHAPTER 4

Hard Work Is a Virtue

One of the most consistent themes I've seen in young women who've turned out to be strong conservatives is that they had jobs when they were young. It's important to encourage your daughter to do the same.

If the Left had its way, Democratic congresswoman from New York Alexandria Ocasio-Cortez would be the pattern after which we would all raise our daughters to think and believe. If that sentence makes you shudder, it should, particularly as it relates to how her radical policy beliefs would irrevocably alter traditional American notions about the value and importance of work.

Consider the Left's "Green New Deal" scheme, which Ocasio-Cortez emphatically advances. It's the perfect symbol for how the Left fundamentally misunderstands the virtue of hard work. Borrowing from President Franklin D. Roosevelt's "New Deal," an explosion of public programs meant to lift the country out of the Great Depression, liberals are attempting to transform society under the guise of environmentalism and climate change. Banning fossil fuels and imposing strict energy mandates on homes and businesses is necessary to shift the United States to an all-renewable energy utopia in ten years, the Left claims. The takeover is so ambitious that even FDR would blush.

Set aside for a moment that a partial transition to renewables in California has led to large-scale electricity blackouts and some of the most expensive utility bills in the country. Crushing costs and suffocating regulations would hollow out business and employment opportunities across America. But Ocasio-Cortez has a plan. A popular socialist and chief advocate of the Green New Deal, Ocasio-Cortez says the government would spend trillions creating new union jobs and providing "economic security for all who are unable or unwilling to work."

"*Unwilling to work*"?! A conservative could never say such a thing. It's unthinkable. Work is about creating value, not just showing up to a job you can't get fired from or collecting an entitlement check. It's critical to teach your daughter the difference. Hard work is central to both the American Dream and personal development. It provides dignity and fulfillment. Work is an opportunity to help others, earn income and support one's family. Conservatives want government out of the way so that individuals can create jobs and opportunity. That's why your daughter must learn the true value of work.

Think about your first job. Does it make you smile? Many adults have fond memories of their first working experiences because they learned to be valuable outside of their family. Whether bagging groceries, waiting tables, mowing yards, or babysitting, people depended on your effort, and they paid for it.

It feels good to earn money and serve others, but it's also an education. When I was 16 years old, I started working at the local movie theatre on weekends as the candy and popcorn–stand girl. Minimum wage was about $1.25, and, after receiving my paycheck, I remember thinking, "What happened?" Taxes had eaten into my tiny check, and it was so disappointing. My dad was right. He spoke about the economy, taxes, and wasteful programs that rarely delivered as promised. Suddenly, those were no longer academic discussions; I was thrust into the real world. But my parents taught me to work hard and fight for what I wanted. The beauty of such lessons is that they set girls up for happiness and success later in life.

Hard Work Is Foundational

Hard work made America great, and it can make your daughter great, too. Our country was built with a can-do spirit and the promise of a better life if you are willing to work for it. Despite the naysayers, that remains true. Opportunities to succeed are more abundant than ever, and girls shouldn't take for granted what they have inherited. In previous generations, most women were expected to be housewives. They took care of children, cooked meals, did the laundry, and kept a lovely home. That was their job, and they were proud because it was hard. Being a housewife is still a wonderful calling, but today women have near-unlimited career choices.

Your daughter will choose her own path. But her success will hinge on her approach to work, and that's mostly learned at home. Parents have different attitudes on the issue, even among conservatives. Some are diligent taskmasters, others are hands-off. Many parents know the value of a job, but they want to protect their children. They fear a job could pull their daughter away from school or expose her to people who don't care for her best interests. Here's the bottom line: whatever your daughter does, she needs to work hard and do her best. In many families, that means getting up early, going to school, getting good grades, excelling at extracurricular activities, and a part-time job—no excuses.

School must come first, because it shapes thinking and brings about the most opportunity. Extracurricular activities and a job are secondary, but still very important. When parents worry about stress and overcommitment, they should look at how their daughter spends time when she's not studying. Many girls waste exorbitant amounts of time, often in unhealthy ways. Yes, children need to rest and enjoy themselves, but idleness, social media excess, and other peer-pressured activities can eat up many hours. Most concerns that come from a job or voluntary service commitment pale in comparison. There's also an expression that, if you want something done, give it to a busy person. That quality will pay huge dividends in life and can develop in childhood where a girl is expected to study and make positive use of her time.

Keep in mind that every job involves a learning curve and a skill set. They also require dealing with people and problem solving. The benefit is that girls start to develop self-reliance and are more apt to avoid the trap of looking for someone to take care of them when they grow up. "If only I can be pretty enough, then I'll find a rich husband." Obviously, little good can come from that. Earning money, developing confidence, and honing people skills will help your daughter forge a more independent path.

Work further teaches personal responsibility. It's a foundational trait for every mature person, though it's often in short supply. There will be times when school, activities, a job, and social desires are in conflict. But making excuses and expecting to be bailed out don't wash, especially when other people are depending on your daughter. Failing to show up and perform at a job, for example, will involve consequences. That's a good thing. Help your daughter face the situation and do her best. Talk with her about accepting responsibility and decision making. And if a situation is painful, support her knowing that she's developing character.

If you put your daughter to work, she's much more likely to turn out conservative. I've seen it over and over again. Girls learn that the things they want aren't going to fall from the sky. They have to earn them. That lesson obliterates helplessness and the entitlement mentality. It also makes them vigilant about government. Conservatives believe that hard work should benefit the worker, not wasteful programs or favored political constituencies. The more time your daughter spends earning, the more government will take. Ask her where she thinks the money is going and if it's well spent. Chances are she will become aware that "government is not the solution to our problem; government is the problem," as President Reagan said. All of a sudden, too-good-to-be-true proposals like the Green New Deal won't be so seductive. Politicians like Alexandria Ocasio-Cortez and Bernie Sanders depend on youthful ignorance, but your daughter will see what's really going on—offering "free" stuff in exchange for freedom.

The Career Mom, Homemaker "Debate"

When discussing the concept of work, it's important to address the discussion in some conservative circles over the decision to be a career mom or a stay-at-home mom or a mix of the two. This is, of course, a deeply personal decision every family must make for themselves. What's more, the liberal media likes to pit one side against the other, as if both sides were adversaries who stood in judgment of each other. Let's cut through the noise.

For many families the decision whether mom works outside the home is purely economic. A one-paycheck income is simply not enough, and therefore mom must earn a paycheck. For those who can afford to choose, some highly successful women put their careers on hold to stay home with their children, while others feel called to continue making an impact at work while raising their kids. Both paths are noble and worthy of respect. Every woman must follow her calling. I do, however, think that some conservatives talk a lot about the virtues of moms staying home and not enough about the virtues of conservative women with careers in public policy and the culture. There is another dimension to family life: the good a woman can do for *all* families and for her country with her work. Let me explain.

When I spent weeks driving across the Commonwealth of Virginia as president of the Virginia State Board of Education for Governor George Allen, I was working to beef up the academic standards taught and then tested for thousands of children in public schools all over Virginia. We shifted the curriculum and testing from social studies to rigorous and truthful history. During those four years I was on the state board of education, my kids and husband missed me, and it was especially hard for me because I had just started the Clare Boothe Luce Center for Conservative Women. But my family knew my time on the road was helping all Virginia kids, not just our own. My kids were always first in my heart, but not every day in my time.

During these state board of education years, I was taping Dr. James Dobson's radio show in Colorado when he was running Focus on the Family. He asked me to be on his show because, since I was a rare conservative woman head of a state board of education, he wanted a conservative woman's insight on some of the key education and family issues. I remember talking with a woman leader at Focus on the Family and telling her that some conservatives criticized me for being out on the road rather than at home. She looked at me and said, "You just tell them God calls us all to serve in different ways," and she commended me for being engaged in public policy for all American families. It was a rare sentiment expressed to me by another Christian, conservative woman.

I also think about conservative icon Jeane Kirkpatrick, former U.S. ambassador to the United Nations. She had four sons. She also made more freedom possible around the world with her intense work schedule and travel. Her family thought her calling and impact were important. It's hard to argue she should have spent more time at home.

Or consider Margaret Thatcher, who spent so much time away from her family helping all Britain's families keep more of their earnings with lower taxes, improving schools, and promoting traditional values. Her kids appreciated what she was doing and understood she was called to fight the corrosive growth of big government confronting her nation's families. She impacted thousands of other children and families, while her own children and husband Dennis did just fine. If Thatcher had spent more time at home, Britain would have been a very different place.

Obviously every girl cannot be prime minister. What I am suggesting is that conservative women in the workforce can have a tremendous impact for good. If all conservative women were at home with no conservative women leaders in the workplace, other left-wing women—of whom there are legions—would fill the vacuum. And it's not just policy careers; conservative women in entertainment and news can make a tremendous impact as well.

It's all about conservative moms—career moms and homemakers—appreciating each other and the unique and important work God has called them each to. Doing so teaches daughters they have an array of options and opportunities. That's a win-win for conservative girls. Whether moms work outside or inside the home, or a mix of both, the key is modeling a strong work ethic.

Role-Modeling Work Ethic

Where does work ethic come from? Most kids learn by watching their parents. For Supreme Court justice Clarence Thomas, it came from his grandfather and a religious school. According to Thomas's autobiography, his father abandoned the family, and his mother couldn't afford him, so his grandfather stepped in and raised him. They lived in the rural South and were very poor. But they worked extremely hard, and young Clarence developed a rock-solid worth ethic at an early age. Thomas also went to a Catholic boarding school where nuns refused to allow a victim mentality and instead pushed him twice as hard to learn. And when other kids played during the summer, he worked outside with his granddad and made extra money.

While away at college, Thomas soured on his upbringing. He became a Marxist revolutionary, which embarrassed his grandfather and Vietnam-veteran brother. Then, despite graduating from law school, he couldn't find a job. Liberal employers steered clear of what they considered affirmative action hires, he said. The only person who extended a hand was a Republican. He was mortified but accepted an offer to work as an assistant attorney general in Missouri. That's when he began to see things differently. "It was one of these road-to-Damascus experiences," he said. By his own account, what he had been told about conservatives wasn't true. Eventually, Thomas would ascend to the highest court in the land and inspire millions of people with his truly American story. But all of it was built on a foundation of hard work.

Imparting work ethic to your daughter is about leadership and being a healthy role model. It's a lot harder for a girl to slack when she knows her parents get up early every day and work to support her. What if dad or mom decided not to go to work today because they didn't feel like it? Proposing such hypotheticals could make for interesting discussions, prompting your daughter to think things through.

I like the way motivational speaker and author Brian Tracy puts it: "Good habits are hard to form, but easy to live with. Bad habits are easy to form, but hard to live with." Children with poor role models suffer. If kids don't see their parents working, it's difficult for them to develop a strong work ethic. They are set up to underperform and fail. And if children are not fortunate enough to grow up and rely on their parents to meet their needs, then government often becomes the provider. Both paths lead to an entitlement trap, which is essentially the belief that you don't have to work to get things, they should just be given to you.

You can imagine how that mentality plays out politically. Shameless politicians promise bigger and bigger benefits, schools supply the narrative that denying them is wrong, and potent constituencies start demanding free stuff as if it were a right instead of something to earn. When successful, new entitlements are accompanied by an increase in government, which saddles the economy with greater taxes and regulation, and the private sphere of life is further reduced. That's how socialism works. It's interesting that conservatives are able to have any success, given that one side of the political spectrum promises to give people things if they vote for them, while the other side says "no." I suspect that work ethic has a lot to do with it. When you are taught the value of work as a child, you are less likely to want your earnings taken away as an adult and handed to people who didn't work for what they want.

Girls with good role models can still have a limited concept of work. At the Clare Boothe Luce Center, we bring in highly successful career women as well as moms who have been at home to share their experiences, and they often dispel notions that success is glamorous and carefree. Whether it's a senator, corporate leader, media star, or scholar, these women invariably talk about how hard they have worked to get where they are. They started working hard when they were very young, and they never stopped. That ethic continues into adulthood, and it can be a real eye-opener for young women who think that they already work hard enough to achieve their dreams. One guest told a room full of girls that she spends hours preparing for her high-profile five-minute news interviews on TV shows. Her message was that nothing worth having comes easy, but that you can achieve great things if you have faith and put in the work.

The Left likes to divorce earning from having to work. But we want to teach our children that it is usually bad when you divorce having income from earning income.

What should parents do when their daughter isn't doing her best? If she's phoning it in at school, not hustling in sports, or just not pulling her weight at home, consequences should follow. Most of the time punishments and rewards go a long way. But setting a good example is still the best way to teach work ethic. Children learn by seeing and then by doing. So, set high standards for yourself and practice what you preach. Then, communicate that everyone in the family has a role to play and that hard work is expected.

A Brief Story

If you want to raise a successful daughter, you are going to have to encourage her work ethic and show her how it pays off. I tell young women that hard work is the minimum and that if they want to get ahead they have to do more than what's expected.

I graduated from college with a degree in psychology with a K–6th grade teaching certificate. My father was adamant that if he helped pay for my college, then I had to graduate and be prepared for a job. That sounds so logical it's almost funny. But there is an approach to higher education today where students are encouraged to indulge their academic whims irrespective of employment considerations. "You go to college to get the education you want." The problem is that many students leave feeling accomplished, only to find out that their six-figure gender studies degree qualifies them for low-level government work or being a coffee shop barista. Rather than accept responsibility for a bad decision, they default to their university training and claim victimhood.

Conservatives typically avoid this mess. But it doesn't mean they are immune to starting at the bottom. My professional journey began as a teacher at an elementary school in Chappaqua, New York. It was a wealthy community, and I was hired as a long-term substitute. Teaching is a wonderful profession, and my dad championed the benefits: you leave at 3:30 p.m., and you get summers off when your kids are home. It made sense. However, after six months I realized it wasn't for me. I came home exhausted and unsatisfied every single day. My new colleagues told me to hang in there, but a small room with twenty-five children wasn't a good fit for me.

I was at a crossroads and decided to make a leap of faith. I had been bitten by the policy bug while previously volunteering for Young Americans for Freedom (YAF), so I packed my bags and moved to Washington, D.C., for a chance to be more involved. You can imagine my dad's reaction when I told him that YAF hired me as a receptionist. I knew I was capable of much more, and there were two ways of looking at the situation: I could get angry and entitled, or I could earn my way up the ladder.

There is nothing wrong with being a receptionist. All honest work deserves respect. But I certainly wasn't satisfied. First, I was grateful for the opportunity. And even though I had to spend a lot of the day answering the phone, I committed to working hard and contributing. That foundation had already been laid. It turns out that the position was a great vantage point to see what was going on. I learned who did what, who had the titles, and who made the important decisions. One day, I heard about a local rock and roll radio station that let people submit editorials and then come in and record them if they were selected. So, I decided to write something. I didn't tell anybody except my coworker Ron, who is today my husband of nearly fifty years.

Sure enough, the station received my letter and invited me to record it. The topic was how the Metro transportation system used to be private, and I argued that private ownership was preferable to government control. Some people in the office heard my report and started calling me. "Was that you on the radio?" "Yes," I told them, "What did you think?" That raised my profile. Next, I wrote about the Equal Rights Amendment. I researched the topic, and it was published as a YAF issue paper. Then I wrote another issue paper ("De-Monopolize the Post Office") that was also published. Shortly after it was published, I received a promotion.

That was the beginning of my career. I started at the bottom and worked my way up to eventually serve twelve consecutive years in the Reagan and then the H. W. Bush administrations. My message to aspiring girls is: you start where you start; you do what's assigned; then, you work late and nights and weekends and do lots more. That's how you move up.

Dos and Don'ts of Teaching Work

There is no perfect way to instill a healthy work ethic in your daughter or to communicate the virtue that flows from it. However, parents can benefit from approaches that help produce desired results. For instance, one of the worst things you can do is complain about your job in front of your daughter. It's easy to vent, and most parents don't realize what they are doing when they say, "I hate my boss," "They don't pay me enough for this grief," or "I'd quit if I could afford it." Even if it's justified, the potential damage can be corrupting. My dad was a business administrator for Harry Guggenheim at the Solemn R. Guggenheim Foundation in my childhood years. There were challenges, but he told his children how he loved his position—and it was good for my three siblings and me to hear that.

Kids learn by listening and watching. And when work is a villain, you create a negative association that can have long-term repercussions.

You are saying work is a necessary evil, not an opportunity and a blessing. Try looking at the glass half-full, or don't say anything. You can also use workplace frustrations as teachable moments and model the behavior you would want from your daughter if she were facing a similar situation. It might be worth praying about or including in a family discussion. Taking a visibly positive approach to adversity can be a powerful testimony.

Parents should also maintain a work-life balance to the best of their ability. Feminism tells girls that they don't need a family, or that marriage and kids can wait because their career should come first. I tell girls that they can be stay-at-home moms or successful working mothers, or a mix of both. It's up to them. But whatever they choose, hard work is required. Housewives are some of the hardest working women I know. There were times while raising my kids when home life on a weekend was so hectic and demanding that I couldn't wait until Monday, because my job was less challenging. At home moms don't have that outlet.

The key is balance, and that can look different ways. You can be a plumber, brain surgeon, or president of the United States, but you don't have to make your daughter an afterthought. Spouses may need to divide family duties and rely on grandparents, if possible. Babysitters, nannies, and other options are often essential, as sacrifices and creative solutions are part of the work-life tension. You may not be able to make every sports game or family dinner, but doing your best, no matter how tired you are, will set an example. Parents who work hard and make their best effort earn the respect of their children. They will know how much you care, especially if the time you spend together is meaningful. You don't need to be parents who flood your daughter with gifts, leaving discipline out. Just work hard, love her, and do your best—the same things you are asking of her.

An allowance is one of the best tools to teach work ethic. It functions like a job. Your daughter does her assigned chores and gets ten dollars a week, for example. Allowance is pretty standard and easy to understand. The point is she has to earn her spending money. Some families are against it and think that children need to do chores without getting paid. There's something to that, but it's important to provide girls with an opportunity to earn the things they want. It's a simple lesson, but not as common as you might think. Many parents can't help themselves from bankrolling shopping sprees for their daughter or letting her dictate what she will and won't do around the house.

Sometimes conflict arises from wanting items that are more expensive than what an allowance affords. You can bridge the gap by offering incentives. If your daughter wants new clothes or a fancy purse, create an add-on list of jobs and projects that involve more responsibility. If she takes on bigger chores, it's only fair to pay more. This is a way to teach growth and reward self-initiative, instead of doling out a set wage for the same tasks, week after week. Add-on options incentivize hard work. Goal-setting and entrepreneurial thinking could also come into play as you work with your daughter to earn the expensive things she wants.

Cars are probably the biggest-ticket item. Some parents roll over and take care of everything. Nothing is asked of their daughter, and there's no lesson or responsibility involved. On the other hand, some think it's unrealistic to deny a car if their daughter is getting good grades and earning enough money to pay for gas and maintenance. I lean toward the school of thought that says no matter how good a child is, parents should wait until their daughter has left the house to allow her to get a car. Call me old-school, but girls can borrow mom or dad's vehicle if they need transportation, and parents can better monitor their daughter's driving while she's a teenager.

Parents should also be careful about reinforcing stereotypes. Boys like trucks and dolls are for girls; I'm all for it. But it's not a good thing when different standards are applied to work. Boys and girls are not the same, but their work ethics should be. Why not assign your daughter yard work and garbage duty once in a while? I can assure you she is capable of more than just laundry and baking cookies. This leads to another important aspect of teaching girls about work: no job is beneath her. Ditch diggers and dishwashers deserve the same respect as investment bankers and corporate executives. Jesus was a carpenter, and his disciples included several fishermen. All honest work is honorable, and sometimes it takes getting our hands dirty for that lesson to sink in. There is another angle to "menial" jobs for the young. One of my sons was very bright but not as serious as he should have been about his schoolwork. A couple of summers working at Target, and he came to realize that without more education he would be stocking shelves forever—this seemed to help motivate him to be more focused on doing better in school.

Whatever your daughter does—with respect to school, activities, a job, and chores—do not let her quit. There are always exceptions, like when her health or safety are at risk, but as a rule quitting is a terrible habit. The impulse usually comes from fear, insecurity, boredom, or frustration, but it's so important to push through. Letting your daughter drop out of a tough situation reinforces the idea that she can give up if something is difficult. Imagine taking that approach with a career or a marriage. Anything worth having is going to come from commitment and hard work. And when adversity strikes, we have to stay strong and move through it. So much of raising a conservative daughter is about teaching responsibility and preventing your girl from tucking tail and running away from hardship. As the saying goes, when the going gets tough, the tough get going. That's the classic American way.

Give your daughter options and let her explore as many opportunities as she wants—and as you can afford. But once she starts something, push her to finish. If you haven't had the experience of a child resisting what they have started, you probably will. And down the road, your daughter will thank you for not letting her off the hook. I can't tell you how gratifying those moments are.

CHAPTER 5

A Woman's Differences Are Her Strengths

Girls are different from boys. That's not just a feeling; it's a biological fact. Most people know this intuitively, but the Left tells parents otherwise. In their quest to condition girls, feminists and liberal educators twist themselves into rhetorical pretzels as they attempt to erase natural variations between the sexes. Ironically, they end up harming women by pushing them to be more like men. The truth is that girls and boys are not the same, and there is nothing wrong with that. A female's differences do not make her weak. They are her strengths.

I see it in my own family. My seven-year-old granddaughter and her twin brother visit every Sunday. I love them dearly, and like so many children they faced unusual challenges in 2020. Their school was forced to close amid the COVID-19 crisis. I noticed they responded in separate ways. The twins were relegated to virtual learning, and my granddaughter spent a great deal of time looking at all of the messages the kids sent to the teacher, whereas her brother simply followed instructions and submitted his work. She needed to see her classmates and missed the social interaction.

Does that make her deficient? No, of course not. It makes her gifted. Research shows that social and emotional learning is healthy for developing girls, but panic-induced school closures harmed them by depriving them of these needs. Social isolation is already commonplace among internet generations, as kids spend more time staring at pixels than peers. And ignoring gender differences only makes it worse.

There are always exceptions, but parents who understand their daughter's innate feminine qualities can better support her and cultivate her long-term potential. Unfortunately, the Left insists on using boys as a measuring stick to decide if girls are ahead or behind in society. It's a misguided approach that casts too narrow a definition on what it means to be a successful woman. Your daughter's femininity is an incredible blessing that's unique unto itself, and it all starts with the power to produce life.

Givers of Life

The biggest difference between women and men is that women give birth. As women we are literally responsible for the survival of the species. Childbearing is a breathtaking miracle that elevates females, yet feminists would have you believe that childbearing is a patriarchal burden that limits success. It's a futile attempt to deny nature.

Women are designed to carry babies for nine months. That affects our bodies and biological choices. We carry one egg per month for a portion of our lives, while men produce hundreds of billions of sperm cells over the course of an average lifetime. That makes us more selective when it comes to choosing sexual partners, while some men are often indiscriminate.

Women are also intimate and tend to bond and fall in love. They want to stay with one man. Marriage represents lifelong security with a mate who will help protect and provide for her children. That leads to another key difference: motherhood. Fathers are essential to raising children, but there is a closeness between mother and child that is truly special. Women carry their babies and birth them. Then, the two cling to one another for months. Even before eyesight develops, newborns find their mothers by smelling their unique scent, and mothers nurse them;

literally sustaining life with their bodies. It's a bond like no other, and the nurturing instinct is a core aspect of femininity.

There is so much dignity in motherhood, so much beauty and strength. Feminists see childrearing as settling for less or a limiting inconvenience that gets in the way of more important career objectives. In a 2020 interview with *The Guardian*, legendary Fleetwood Mac liberal singer Stevie Nicks said this about her decision to abort her child: "If I had not had that abortion, I'm pretty sure there would have been no Fleetwood Mac. There's just no way that I could have had a child then, working as hard as we worked constantly." She went on to say that she knew the music she would make would "heal so many people's hearts and make people so happy." So, Nicks says, "I thought: you know what? That's really important. There's not another band in the world that has two lead women singers, two lead women writers. That was my world's mission." What a heartbreaking outlook on so many levels.

The establishment media, aided by far-left tech giants like Google, would have you believe that abortion regret is a myth. Just Google the phrase "abortion regrets" and you'll see how Google pushes propaganda masquerading as "research" from Leftist pro-abortion groups and left-leaning publishers to the top of its search results. They do this because they know that very few people—particularly young people with limited attention spans—will click far beyond the first few search results. It's sickening and alarming, which is why parents must help their daughters understand the manipulation. But the truth is that many women who have had abortions look back with deep sadness and regret, and those who chose not to abort their babies later experience gratitude for the blessings their children bring them.

I'm talking about young women like *American Idol* contestant Kimberly Henderson, who considered having an abortion but changed her mind in the abortion clinic. As she explained in a moving Facebook post that went viral worldwide: "I had my mind made up. My boyfriend was cheating on me...I kept telling myself, "I'm all alone; I need to do this." Sitting there...I could hardly make out anyone or anything through the tears. I kept telling and giving myself every reason to go through with this even though I did not believe in it." Then, says Henderson, she told a woman at the clinic that she changed her mind. "As I was about to walk out, a young girl no older than probably 19 says to me, 'Are you going to do it?' I told her I couldn't. She said, 'I wish I could be brave like you.'...She said she had to do it become of some serious circumstances. As I turned around she said, 'When you see your baby's face for the first time you're gonna be so glad you walked out of here today.'"[1] Henderson says her decision to have her daughter Vaida has given her endless joy and love. She wrote a song called "Tiny Hearts" in tribute that went to number five on iTunes.

As women, we are givers of life. Encourage your daughter to know she must also be a defender and champion of life, too.

Behavior and Choices

There are also behavioral differences between women and men, and some of them are related to physical characteristics. Men have testosterone, for example, and it tends to make them more aggressive. Not that women can't be aggressive, but it's more of a nurture-over-nature quality. I've known about female lawyers who are very tough, and some rub testosterone cream on their pulse points before going into trial because it spikes their aggressiveness.

Men are much more likely to engage in dangerous activities and physically target other men. Prison populations are overwhelmingly male for these reasons. Women can certainly be reckless and violent, but they don't act that way as often.

We have all heard that women are "emotional." Sometimes that's used as a put-down. I don't see it that way. First, feelings aren't bad; they don't make girls weak. They tell us what is going on inside and help us have fuller life experiences. Second, many men are just as emotional, but they don't show it as much as women. That's in part due to how boys and girls are conditioned. "Real men don't cry," boys are told. There is nothing wrong with showing emotion, and it's perfectly fine to raise your daughter to be feminine and tough as nails.

There aren't any meaningful differences between men and women when it comes to intelligence, but there are some performance variations in certain areas. For instance, it's not uncommon for girls to have better linguistic abilities. If you notice this trait in your daughter, encourage her oratorical talents instead of telling her that she talks too much. Studies show that men and women can process language differently. Men tend to use the left side of their brains for linguistic tasks, while women use both sides. Conversely, men fare better at spatial visualization tasks and mathematics. That doesn't mean women can't succeed in these areas or that your daughter shouldn't pursue physics or become a fighter pilot. It means performance patterns show that men and women are often geared differently.

Parents should beware of agendas that seek to exploit natural variations in male/female outcomes. Without looking at why men gravitate toward computer programming or why women thrive as elementary school teachers, misogyny and discrimination narratives can sweep in and explain away meaningful differences. As conservatives, we want equal opportunity for girls, not forced outcomes driven by politics. That said, if your daughter is genuinely trapped beneath a glass ceiling, I would encourage you to take action. By all means, teach her to fight back and support her throughout any process where she has been denied her equal protection under the law. But where claims of sexism and wrongdoing aren't warranted, teach your daughter not to take the easy way out. It's so easy to be a victim these days.

Don't Be Fooled

Perhaps the biggest example of how benign differences and choices are exploited in the workplace is the "wage gap" myth. It's proof that if you repeat a lie over and over again, eventually people will think it's true. The wage gap is the idea that women are paid less than men. If a woman and a man do the same job, somehow a woman will come up short because she's female. It's a liberal myth. It's just not true. It may have been true at one time, and there are always exceptions, but those days are long gone. Studies show that among similarly situated young men and women with equal education, family obligations, and experience, women are sometimes paid more!

It's commonly stated that women make seventy-seven to eighty-two cents for every dollar a man makes, depending on variables. The figures come from simply dividing the average salary for women by the average salary for men. The number always comes out lower for women, and sexism and discrimination are the stated cause. What goes unmentioned, however, are the voluntary decisions that many women make. For example, some women choose to drop out of the workforce when they have children. Most come back, but some don't. Some women limit their aspirations and career choices to afford more time with their families. That's their choice, but it obviously cuts a woman's earnings and time building career seniority.

Women are also known to choose college majors that don't command top dollar. The social services fields and K–12 education jobs are dominated by women. They are tremendously important, and it takes a special person to serve others in these positions. But they don't pay as much as engineering, legal, or medical professions. They also don't pay as much as more dangerous professions, such as oil rig or lineman jobs, either. That's nobody's fault; it's free market capitalism. It's worth discussing these realities with your daughter *before* she goes to college, and prior to the bills' coming home. Remind her that a gender studies degree will lead to less lucrative employment opportunities than many other majors.

Parents should help their daughter identify her passions and then support her as she makes choices. Whatever that looks like, arm her with knowledge about phony victim narratives like the wage gap that only serve to pull women away from realizing their potential. The best way to do that is to instill the idea that she is ultimately responsible for her own success.

Feminism Is Not the Standard

Parents need to know what they are up against. Feminism and women's studies programs teach girls that, no matter how smart or hardworking they are, the world is stacked against them because they are female. The argument goes something like this: "If you are a woman, you are disadvantaged because of men who promote the patriarchy. You are a victim, and men are the obstacle you have to overcome." It's such nonsense. Liberals are discouraging girls from being their best. We live in the most free and prosperous country in the world. To tell women that they cannot succeed in their career without the government's help is absurd.

It makes me angry when the Left indoctrinates girls with this poison and then tears down women who succeed without embracing feminism. Hillary Clinton was praised for her *Book of Gutsy Women*, which she co-authored with her daughter Chelsea. When asked why conservative Prime Minister Margaret Thatcher wasn't included among their gutsy-lady portrayals, Hillary said Thatcher didn't meet the definition of her book, which was "knocking down barriers for others and trying to make a positive difference." The Iron Lady didn't knock down barriers? Get real. That's just willful self-deception.

And what about Supreme Court justice Amy Coney Barrett? Just thinking about her makes me smile. Justice Barrett represents everything that a traditional woman can aspire to be. She's brilliant, happy, highly accomplished, and so much more. She earned her way to the U.S. Supreme Court while remaining a devoted wife, devout Christian, and mother of seven children. Forgive me, but I have to repeat that—*seven* children! Justice Barrett should be a celebrated heroine for every girl who dreams of having a family and a successful career when she grows up. And yet, the Left tears her down.

I went to college in the late 1960s and saw the rise of feminism firsthand. I lived through it, and parents could benefit from recognizing how it works. Radical feminists are largely opposed to marriage and family, and their way of thinking is hostile to classic femininity. They are at war with the most beautiful aspects of being a woman and want to reorder nature. Feminism gained traction as part of the anti-Vietnam movement and anti-establishment era, when feminists took the original women's suffrage platform and redirected it for left-wing political ends. Suffrage was about equal treatment under the law. But they pushed a partisan agenda that continues to harm girls today. "If it feels good, do it." That was the mantra of the feminist sexual revolution. Women were told to discard morality because it was patriarchal oppression. You might recognize modern offshoots like the "nasty" women with pink hats symbolizing their private parts who opposed President Donald Trump in so-called resistance marches. Do not let your daughter fall for such lunacy.

The early feminist radicals weren't martyrs who sacrificed to make the world a better place. Many, like Andrea Dworkin, had an axe to grind. Dworkin was unlucky in love. Her father was also a committed socialist whom she credited with inspiring her activism. Sadly, she claims she married an abusive husband when she was young. What followed was man-hating. Women who don't attract the attention of men, or who experience emotional or physical abuse, are left wondering, "Why?" An easy answer is that men are evil. Well, they are not. The vast majority of men aren't bad; that's a fact. Gloria Steinem is another prominent example of a man-hating woman. She remains an A-list feminist icon known for calling marriage an institution that destroys women. Ironically (or hypocritically), she became a first-time bride at age sixty-six. Notably, the woman who performed Steinem's ceremony was a Native American literally named Wilma Mankiller.

The 1960s may seem like ancient history to young women. But these radicals were the originators of ideas that your daughter will likely encounter at some point, whether online, at school, or through entertainment. The simplest way to explain feminism to your daughter now is that it's selfish. And selfishness leads to an unfulfilled life.

Selfishness Leads to Loneliness

You may have heard of the hit television show *Sex and the City*. It was a long-running HBO comedy-drama that celebrated the sexual exploits of a group of professional women living in New York City. The lead character was a "sex columnist" who wrote about Manhattan's posh dating scene. Glamour, success, and promiscuity highlighted a seductive world with few consequences. The show was adapted from a book by author Candace Bushnell, whose career closely resembled her work of feminist fiction. Years later, Bushnell admitted she had made a terrible mistake. "When I was in my 30s and 40s, I didn't think about it," she said in an interview. "Then when I got divorced and I was in my 50s, I started to see the impact of not having children and of truly being alone."

My heart goes out to women who take the lonely road. It's tragic. Feminist temptations are powerful, but the price is high. Your daughter will be told that she can put her selfish desires first and that it's her right to do so; she just has to be strong enough. Well, no. She can't be selfish if she wants to live a full and happy life. Even conservative girls are susceptible. They talk about the careers they want and plan them straight through their prime family-making years. "First, I need to graduate from college. Then, I'll pay off my student loans. I'll come back and go to law school, work my way up the ladder for a few years, get financially settled, and then think about a family." I ask them, how old will you be when you are finally ready for a family, and what happens if you fall in love along the way? You can't just find the man you want to marry when it's convenient. That's not how life works. A few of these great young conservative leaders I've worked with over the years have fallen into this trap; they wait and wait and wait.

There is nothing wrong with taking care of yourself and pushing for a successful career, but girls have to be open to the other things in life that matter. That's where *Sex and the City* goes off the rails. It's a have-your-cake-and-eat-it-too approach to being a woman. But it doesn't take marriage, motherhood, and family into account. And it sweeps another key difference with men under the rug, which is that women are not able to have children forever. Fertility begins to decline at age thirty, and declines quite dramatically at thirty-five. The window of opportunity eventually closes. Waiting until it's too late results in a devastating realization that I pray your daughter never experiences.

Make sure your daughter knows that life isn't all about her. It's common sense, but girls are bombarded with self-centered, consequence-free messaging from media, celebrities, politicians, and educators. "It's all about you, and the most important thing is to do what feels good." There's no room in that perspective for sacrifice and service. It's entirely me, me, me. We want girls to be confident and educated, and they should feel empowered to pursue successful careers. But they have to understand that a "me-first" attitude is a road to nowhere. Without love and family, life is a long, lonely journey.

Parents who wish to steer their daughters away from regret can show a better alternative at home. That means a healthy marriage, family, hard-working careers, and lots of love. Make sure to teach your daughter that being feminine and strong is both wise and attractive, and that marriage and motherhood are worthy aspirations, not something a girl settles for.

Let Girls Be Girls

Conservative girls are generally raised to want children. It's intuitive for most women to want kids. Little girls carry toy babies and play with dolls out of instinct. If there's a truck, they often make it into a little person and talk to it. I see this with my granddaughter, and I'm amazed. She and her twin brother are treated the same, and yet she talks to her toys, whereas he would rather launch a truck across the room than have a conversation with it.

Still, inappropriate and dangerous role modeling gets pushed further and further into the mainstream every day. Conservatives and people of faith have always been wary of such influences, but technological advances and easy access to troubling subject matter raises new concerns. Netflix, the online movie-streaming giant, is in nearly every American household. The company has also been cited for "lewd visual material" involving young girls. The recent controversy stems from a film called *Cuties*, where an eleven-year-old main character leaves her traditional family to join a "free-spirited dance crew." She and other girls are hyper-sexualized in a way that resembles adult entertainment. That's not a stuffy exaggeration. Despite backlash, Netflix has refused to back down from the film's "creative expression."

Cuties is one of many examples of what girls are facing these days. Parents have to be vigilant and protect their daughters from predatory influences. The other side of the coin is that they need to allow space for their daughter to grow. So your daughter isn't a girly-girl. Some girls are tomboys, and they would rather climb trees and make mudpies than play with Barbies. That's fine! Allow your daughter to be who God made her to be.

Girls move through phases. Today's tomboy may be tomorrow's beauty queen. You never know what's around the corner with kids, and that's part of the fun. The point is for parents to protect their girls and trust their natural development. Allow your daughter's femininity to blossom in God's perfect timing.

This used to be well-understood, but there is so much emphasis today on gender. Today people are obsessed with the false notion that your biological sex doesn't determine whether you are a boy or a girl. It is now controversial to say, "boys don't wear dresses" or "only girls can menstruate." Biology isn't a game, yet some liberal parents are taking extraordinary risks by tinkering with nature. I call it politically correct child abuse. Conservative parents are the only bulwark against those who want to make bizarre gender-bending hormonal treatments more accessible for minors. Those treatments can inflict permanent reproductive damage on girls, and parents have to be aware of such malevolent forces while raising their girls to be girls.

Dating and Intimacy

Dr. Miriam Grossman is a woman very knowledgeable in her field. She is a medical doctor with training in pediatrics and child, adolescent, and adult psychiatry. She has also served as a physician at UCLA's Student Counseling Services for more than twelve years. There, Dr. Grossman helped young women cope with the consequences of "hook-up culture." Broken hearts, genital infections, one or more abortions, exposure to HIV, and other devastating cases of promiscuous-activity-gone-wrong have flooded her office over the years. All of it adds up to regret, and the worst part is almost every case could have been prevented.

Dr. Grossman's experiences have led her to speak out against political correctness on campus and in the medical community, which she says has caused great harm to girls. Her booklet, *Sense and Sexuality: The College Girl's Guide to Real Protection in a Hooked-up World*, written when she worked and was paid as a Clare Boothe Luce Fellow, is posted on the Clare Boothe Luce Center website. In it, she warns young women about poor choices: "Hardly a day has gone by without my meeting a young woman like you.... But she's in crisis, and there are lots of tears as she shares her struggles and setbacks. I feel terrible, but there's not much I can do." By the time they seek her help, it's too late. The girls can't go back and make a different choice. And the number one response she receives from teary-eyed girls is that they didn't know the risks of their behavior.

That's where parents can help—before tragedy strikes and dreams are derailed. Hook-up culture teaches girls that "anything goes" and that you should just try to use protection, and girls are told to get tested regularly for STDs. Promiscuity is viewed as a right, rather than a choice with serious risks, and disagreement is seen as judgment. It will be hard for your daughter to go against the grain, but parents have to take the approach that no one is going to protect their child better than they will. So, give her reasons not to compromise her body.

Start with science. For example, a younger cervix is more vulnerable to infection. Also, many sexually active boys don't know that they have transmittable diseases like herpes and HPV because they don't show obvious symptoms. Condoms also have significant failure rates, and STDs can cause long-term damage like ovarian cancer and infertility. Throw in alcohol and impaired decision-making, and girls are just asking for trouble. These aren't overstated scenarios. They happen every day along with unexpected pregnancies and other preventable problems. Ask you daughter, "Are they worth it?"

Tell her that it doesn't have to be that way, and that the goal should be to save herself for marriage. That may be a tall order; it may seem weird if she hasn't heard it before in church. But the immediate benefits are clear: a 100 percent chance of not getting pregnant or contracting a sexually transmitted disease. It's also important to explain why waiting is a worthy aspiration. Your daughter isn't likely to hear about it anywhere else except for in a religious environment or in your home. So, take care to explain that marriage is a union of two souls, and sex is a gift that helps bond them together. Yes, it feels good and allows for procreation, but sexual intimacy reinforces trust and attachment, which is cheapened in premarital hook-up culture. That's why women feel used and unfulfilled after a one-night stand.

Girls who fall short should not be condemned. And they can start fresh again, at any time. None of us is perfect, and we all deserve grace. The idea is to communicate good information and reinforce it with positive examples. Waiting until you are married, or just not basing a relationship on sex, doesn't mean your daughter is going to be a social outcast. It means she's making good decisions that will benefit her for life. That's a strong selling point for girls who need a different vision than what's offered on campus or from Hollywood.

Studies show that couples who have sex early in their relationships face greater hurdles, because they don't prioritize the things that make relationships work. Waiting encourages developing trust and interpersonal skills such as listening and communication. Studies also show that couples who wait longer to have sex are more likely to have happier, more stable relationships, and that waiting until marriage has significantly greater outcomes, including higher-quality intimacy.

Your daughter is too special to cheapen her body. She knows this, but parents have to take measures to counter harmful influences that lead girls astray. I tell girls that the most important decision they will make in their adult lives is whom they are going to marry and that waiting for that person for intimacy only helps them make the right call. You want to marry someone who respects you, someone you can grow and raise a family with. Purity is not a punishment. It's a protection that will cement a relationship around the things that matter.

Taking Charge

Women are not the weaker sex. They are separate and unique from men, and their differences are their strengths. Women are the givers of life. They make independent choices based on biology and self-determined priorities. Women are not victims simply by virtue of being female. On the contrary, they have great power, and parents should guard their daughters against destructive feminist ideologies.

Teach your daughter at an early age to respect her femininity. One of the best exercises is to focus on her self-presentation. She doesn't have to look like the church lady character, but the way she dresses sends an important message to her and to others. Modesty, as they say, is the best policy. This also applies to teenagers and college girls. If they are dressing inappropriately, talk to them. Let them know that they are inviting unhealthy attention and that they deserve to be treated with respect. We created a fund at the Clare Booth Luce Center to take girls shopping so they could experience the pride that goes along with enhancing femininity and professionalism. The idea was to support their natural gifts—and there are many ways parents can do that.

Above all, show your daughter that it's healthy to grow up, get married, have a fulfilling and successful career, and have children. Conservative women do it every day. With your guidance and support, there is nothing that can stop your daughter from realizing her dreams.

CHAPTER 6

Defend Life

Over 60 million innocent babies have been eliminated by abortion since the 1973 *Roe v. Wade* decision. It's hard to grasp the enormity of the human carnage that entails. So let's put it in terms your daughter can more easily relate to.

60 million is more than the state populations of California and New York *combined.*

60 million dead babies is the equivalent death toll of a 9/11 terrorist attack happening every day for 54 years straight. Imagine that: 54 years where every single day a 9/11 terrorist attack–sized death toll (3,000) takes place. Such figures defy human comprehension.

After 9/11, America launched the Iraq War, which cost an estimated $2 trillion and 7,014 U.S. military lives, as well as another 7,950 U.S. contractor deaths. And yet, every single day in America, a war is waged inside the womb that claims the most innocent and defenseless among us—the unborn. Unlike the War on Terror, the daily killing of innocent children does not dominate headlines, appear on nightly newscasts reporting the daily casualty figures, or consume floor debates in the United States House and Senate. Instead, we are expected to go about our days as if everything is normal. But it's not. It's wrong. And it's up to us as parents to teach our children the truth.

Life is precious. Yet, there is a powerful lobby dedicated to snuffing out innocent lives in the womb. It's a monstrous practice mostly based on convenience, and there is no moral wiggle room for those who embrace it. As Mother Teresa once said during her sainted lifetime mission of mercy for the poor, "The greatest misery of our time is the generalized abortion of children." President Ronald Reagan echoed her sentiment in a book called *Abortion and the Conscience of the Nation*, where he explained, "The real question today is not when human life begins, but what is the value of human life?"

When parents impart that a girl's worth flows from God, and when girls are taught to respect themselves and their life-giving bodies, they will know that life is sacred and must be defended. Conservatives believe that we must be a voice for the voiceless. Children are taught in school to protect animals and the environment. There are fines and jail sentences for disturbing bird nests and turtle eggs, or harming wolves, whales, and spotted owls. But when it comes to protecting babies with beating hearts from being hacked to pieces and sucked out with vacuums, liberals remain fiercely committed to keeping the practice legal and easy to obtain.

Conservative daughters know that abortion is the taking of an innocent human life, plain and simple. It destroys a baby and damages women and their families. A strong, smart, conservative girl must learn to stand up and speak out for the rights of the unborn. She must defend those who cannot defend themselves.

Damage, Regret, and the Abortion Lobby

A tsunami of money and propaganda is aimed at convincing young women that disposing of their babies in utero is not only a right, but completely normal and carefree. According to its 2019 annual report, abortion giant Planned Parenthood has net assets valued at just under

$2 billion ($1.993 billion).[1] The pro-abortion Alan Guttmacher Institute has an annual budget of $19 million. The National Abortion and Reproductive Rights Action League (NARAL) reported total 2019 revenues of $12,776, 633.[2] In 2018, the National Abortion Federation reported total expenses of $9,788,281.[3] EMILY'S List, a group that funds pro-abortion candidates and whose acronym means "Early Money Is Like Yeast," raised $110 million in 2018 alone.[4] On and on it goes. The big money pro-abortion industry sends its tidal wave of cash crashing into American public policy and the nation's girls, with little regard for what abortion leaves in its wake.

Abortions haunt women for the rest of their lives, and a botched abortion can destroy a young woman's ability to have children. There will always be a feeling of wondering what her child would have been like if she had made a different decision. Even if she is still able to have children later, the haunting pain remains. What would he or she be like today? Maybe a woman has sons, but not a baby girl. She may wonder if the child she aborted years ago would have been her daughter. I've heard the heart-wrenching stories. Losing a child in any scenario is earth-shattering. I know. I lost a daughter to heart surgery.

Conservatives do not wish these women harm, only grace. And parents can help their daughter understand the value of life in many positive ways. For example, expose her to women like Rachel Campos-Duffy, a successful speaker and TV commentator, who has spoken many times to the young women at the Clare Boothe Luce Center. Rachel has eight beautiful children, and when she learned that her ninth child would have special needs, she still believed this baby was a gift from God. When her daughter Valentina was born, Rachel called her the sweetest, most perfect angel she had ever seen. What an incredible role model. There are many women who refused to abort their children when others told them they should. Their stories are inspiring, especially when told by the children whose lives were saved. Life is a gift from God and as a result must be protected.

At the height of the Cold War, Pope John Paul II visited our nation's capital and shared the same reverence for life with America. I was days from having my first child, and I remember the pope describing Westerners in the modern world as focused on creature comforts. It remains a relevant message. We want to give our children everything: clothes, cars, vacations, toys, the list goes on. But the greatest gift parents can give their children, he said, is siblings.

If you have a brother or sister, or multiple siblings, imagine going through life without them. Kids squabble over little things when they are young, but they are an amazing blessing to each other. The idea of robbing a child of these lifelong blood relationships through an abortion is so sad. Yet it happens every day, or actually every ninety-seven seconds at America's largest abortion provider, Planned Parenthood.[5] If parents think pro-abortionists are going to sit idly while they teach their daughter to defend life, they should think again. Pro-abortion forces are as determined as they are extreme.

In 2019, supposedly moderate Democrats showed how extreme they are on abortion when a Virginia state legislator proposed a bill that would radically alter the state's laws concerning late term abortions. And the proposed bill wasn't just supported by a backbench state politician. The next day, Virginia governor Ralph Northam—a pediatrician by training—advocated for abortion after delivery, or infanticide. "...If a mother is in labor, I can tell you exactly what would happen. The infant would be delivered. The infant would be kept comfortable. The infant would be resuscitated if that's what the mother and the family desired, and then a discussion would ensue between the physicians and the mother," he said during an interview.

This moral darkness is a kind of depravity no civilized nation can tolerate. The Left's disregard for life is jaw-dropping, and the damage such policies causes women is incalculable. Abortion is the elimination of an innocent life, and its promotion creates a climate of violence in our society that many ignore. Ripping a baby from its mother limb by limb, or heaven forbid the snuffing out of a life after birth, is nothing short of barbaric. And why? Because the baby is inconvenient?

Did you know that sex-selective abortions, which typically target unborn girls, are defended by the pro-abortion community? Parents might assume that since "abortion on demand" is a left-wing position, and that feminism is also a left-wing phenomenon, that aborting a baby simply because it's a girl would be soundly opposed. Not so. According to the pro-abortion Alan Guttmacher Institute, "bans on sex-selective abortions place a burden on providers," and "while disguised as a means to eliminate gender discrimination, [anti-sex-selective] laws make abortion less accessible." Such depravity is senseless to those who value life.

Teaching the Sanctity of Life

No matter how much money and influence the abortion lobby has, it cannot change the fact that taking an innocent life is morally wrong. Still, killing babies is a big business. As we've seen, pro-abortion forces spend lavishly on political campaigns and legislative agendas. They also play words games such as calling abortion "women's health care." And they employ politically correct language to pander to "social justice" groups by claiming that legal restrictions on abortion is discrimination against women or a tool of oppression against minorities. Parents must teach their daughters the truth.

Parents can also take heart that younger generations are increasingly sensitive to human rights, and people cannot embrace "human rights" and abortion at the same time. The two are incompatible. Explain to your daughter that all life is precious. One of the reasons the pro-abortion side refuses to call an unborn child a baby is because they can't concede the moral absolute that every human being has a right to life. That's why they rephrase abortion as "reproductive health," as if pro-lifers are standing in the way of basic health care. It's nonsense.

Claiming an unborn child is not a human life also goes against science. Make sure your daughter understands that. Liberals act as if they have a monopoly on science, and that pro-lifers are backwards Bible thumpers. Explaining scientific facts will help your daughter differentiate good information from bad. For example, human life does not begin at birth or late-stage pregnancy, it begins when a male sperm cell penetrates a female ovum and a zygote is created. A zygote is the first cell formed at the miracle of conception and is the earliest developmental stage of the human embryo.

A zygote has a unique genetic composition that is totally distinct from its mother, DNA unique from anyone else in human history. This is a crucial point for the battlefield of ideas, because a leading pro-abortion argument is that a baby is not an independent person, but a part of the mother. From there, it's a short jump to justifying an abortion.

But an embryo is a human being, not just a "clump of cells." An unborn baby's heart begins beating very early during pregnancy, and they can survive outside of the mother—and eventually thrive—at just twenty-two weeks of gestation. Life is sustainable by a pregnancy's second trimester, and it has been demonstrably proven that unborn babies feel pain.

In addition to ethical and scientific considerations, parents can help their daughter uphold the sanctity of life by dispelling common myths. For example, pro-life supporters are often accused of hypocrisy if they support the death penalty. "How can you claim to be 'pro-life' and support the death penalty? You don't believe all life matters; you're a hypocrite!" But the difference is clear: an unborn baby is an innocent human being; a convicted murderer is not. The same goes for the military. U.S. armed forces attack those who wish to attack America and Americans. Defending innocent life is the opposite of murder. Don't let your girl fall for the Left's lazy logic.

There are volumes of philosophical and religious literature dedicated to these arguments. But to offer an example, Osama bin Laden was not an innocent human being. Neither were Adolf Hitler and Ted Bundy. They made horrific choices that warranted justice. An unborn child, however, has committed no crime or terrorist act. Babies never declared war against our country; rather, parts of our country declared war against babies. As President Reagan once put it, "I've noticed that everyone who is for abortion has already been born."

Ask your daughter if it's acceptable to allow a defenseless person to be harmed. Then ask about babies in the womb. When parents explain the fundamental problems with abortion, their daughters will know right from wrong.

Google and Miseducation

Parents cannot rely on far-left tech companies like Google, or the public education system to teach girls the conservative side of controversial issues, especially abortion. The media and internet giants weight the scales in favor of the pro-abortion side much more heavily than you may realize.

Google is the gateway to the internet. About 90 percent of all internet searches in the United States run through Google, which deliberately ranks certain news and information, while suppressing other sources and views. Google once ranked results in a content neutral way, relying on popularity and credibility among other internet users.

But in the recent past, Google decided to rank information based on political content. Webpages that don't support the narrative Google wants to advance disappear. Information that was once readily accessible is increasingly difficult to find. Guess which side pro-life websites fall on.

Here's a quick experiment: try to search for the number of aborted babies since the *Roe v. Wade* decision in 1973. Simply "Googling" it will get you the number but will also likely turn up pro-choice articles and sketchy "fact-checks" undermining the figures. When looking for quality research material, encourage your daughter to visit pro-life websites like the www.nrlc.com for the National Right to Life organization, www.focusonthefamily.com/prolife, www.studentsforlife.org, www.liveaction.org, and www.sba-list.org for the Susan B. Anthony List website.

Liberals have the luxury of relying on the news media and public school systems to make their case, but conservative parents have to teach their daughters to defend life on their own. Conservatives have to know their arguments inside and out and have the courage to stand up and speak out. That can be challenging, *but it's also empowering!*

Arm Your Daughter with Pro-Life Arguments

Years ago, when I was in law school at American University, a group of activist girls cornered me in the ladies' room. They put me on the spot about abortion. It's something girls did then, and I'm certain it's worse now. Their objective wasn't to persuade me, but to bully me into changing my position. But I didn't back down. I had been raised to fight, and I knew my arguments. I held my ground, and they eventually withdrew, one by one. It was a confidence-building experience I have never forgotten.

Girls should take a similar approach to handling political bullies. They should learn to confront idealogues with tenacity and grace. And it doesn't take that much in the way of facts to be successful. As conservative Luce speaker Bay Buchanan likes to say, if a conservative girl knows five key facts on a social issue and can explain herself, she can usually beat a liberal student in a debate, because Leftist kids generally only know one or two.

For example, when someone claims that a woman has the right to do whatever she wants with her body, your daughter can explain that an unborn baby is a totally separate body. It gestates within the mother, but it's not her property—it's a person. That's why we ask pregnant women if they are having a boy or a girl, not "how's your fetus?" We also throw pregnant mothers baby showers, not fetus showers.

Your daughter can appeal to science, as previously discussed, or simply refer to advances in prenatal technology that clearly depict babies in the womb. Abortion supporters are terrified of 4D ultrasound images because they remove all doubt that a child in the mother is virtually the same as a child outside of the mother. Even small children understand this when they see modern prenatal pictures. There is nowhere for abortionists to go rhetorically speaking, other than just to claim a right to kill a baby. That's not something they want to admit.

Finally, to the "a-woman-can-do-whatever-she-wants-with-her-own-body" argument, your daughter should be prepared to point out that many U.S. laws rightfully restrict humans from "doing whatever they want with their own body." For example, it's illegal to use your body to kill an innocent person. It's also illegal in most places in the U.S. to "use your body" to make money through prostitution, selling narcotics, or robbing a bank. The point is that the law places limits on "what a person can do with her body" all the time, and for good reason.

Another argument is that pro-life protections will lead to back-alley or "coat-hanger" abortions. The reality, of course, is that many abortion clinics are themselves a threat to a woman's health—and certainly the life and health of the baby. In the quest to make the practice as accessible as possible, the pro-choice lobby often resists imposing even elementary medical safety standards. According to the pro-life Susan B. Anthony List, abortion clinics across the country fail health inspections and harm women every year. The organization notes that "vile conditions are endemic to the abortion industry as a whole."

Those who defend life are also accused of resigning women to poverty, since their lives would be interrupted by keeping a child they don't want. But that's not true, either. There are many counseling and support services for women who struggle, and there are huge numbers of people who would happily adopt and care for a mother's unwanted child. It's a false dichotomy to say a woman must live in misery or abort her baby. Make sure your daughter understands this, and remind her that churches, civic organizations, and good people all over the country are interested in helping struggling moms no matter where they fall on the economic ladder.

Arresting women and throwing them in jail for having an abortion is another favorite straw man argument that's meant to portray legal restrictions on abortions as scary and cruel. In reality, no serious person wants to put a woman in jail for an abortion. First, if a woman has one where it's legal, then putting her behind bars is an impossibility. No laws would be broken. But that clear logic may not register in an emotionalized debate. Your daughter should be prepared to knock down the Left's hollow arguments so she can defend and protect the rights of unborn babies.

The trickiest point your daughter is likely to encounter is that pregnancies should be terminated in cases of incest and rape. Pro-abortion advocates use this argument to make pro-life advocates seem radical and insensitive. It's also used as a foot-in-the-door argument, where conceding abortions on this issue opens the door for further concessions.

I realize this may seem controversial, but one act of violence does not justify another act of violence. Perpetrators of rape or incest should be held accountable to the fullest extent of the law. Period. But ripping a baby apart limb by limb from its mother will only compound the tragedy. Research shows that many women experience psychological trauma, flashbacks, and PTSD long after they abort their babies. Adding that pain to an already horrific situation is not necessary. Someone else can care for the child if need be. Thankfully, these situations are few and far between. Indeed, according to the Centers for Disease Control (CDC), rape-related pregnancies (RRP) are a tiny fraction of pregnancies in the United States.[6] Really, the pro-abortionists are just trying to create a huge antilife loophole where anyone can get an abortion by claiming a rape.

Finally, under no circumstances should taxpayer money ever pay for abortions, whether at home or abroad. If your daughter is confronted about abortion as a form of health care—or perhaps a craven form of population control—and that taxpayer resources should subsidize such health services, she can argue that abortion is the taking of an innocent life. No taxpayer should ever have to pay for that. It's morally offensive. And it directly defies the pro-abortion claim of being "pro-choice."

In a later chapter, we'll talk more about the finer points of teaching your daughter effective communication and debate skills. But the first step is knowing her way around the common arguments pro-abortion forces throw out and how best to defeat them. And no organization does more to ram pro-abortion arguments down Americans' throats than Planned Parenthood.

Planned Parenthood

Planned Parenthood is the tip of the spear for the pro-abortion lobby. It's flush with funding, consists of more than six hundred clinics around the country, and is aggressively political. It enjoys the support of powerful donors and politicians, and the establishment media are quick to deflect controversy while amplifying its messaging. All of that, combined with campus feminism, is aimed at your daughter. But parents need only show the origins of the organization and how its mission continues to this day to undermine Planned Parenthood's cacophony of misinformation.

Planned Parenthood comes from the early twentieth-century eugenics movement. Its founder, Margaret Sanger, was a known racist and eugenicist. She was also a die-hard liberal who believed that sterilizing "the feeble minded" and promoting "birth control" would stem "the rising stream of the unfit." Sanger aligned with segregationists and even the Ku Klux Klan while pushing sinister programs like the "Negro Project," which attempted to reduce the black population in the American South. In a rare moment of honesty for the pro-abortion movement, amid the 2020 racial unrest in America, Planned Parenthood of Greater New York (PPGNY) announced its intent to remove Margaret Sanger's name from its building due to her "harmful connections to the eugenics movement."[7]

These are facts the Left tries to sweep under the rug. It's also just the tip of the iceberg when it comes to the organization's disturbing past. Parents won't find any direct references on Planned Parenthood's website. Its version of history begins like this: "Planned Parenthood traces its roots back to nurse, educator[,] and founder Margaret Sanger—whose activism changed the world. Sanger had the revolutionary idea that women should control their own bodies—and thus their own destinies.

Imagine that!" There's a reason Planned Parenthood plays rhetorical games over its history and founding: the more girls know the truth about Margaret Sanger, the less likely they are to be wooed by the abortion giant's propaganda.

Teach your daughter the truth. It may be helpful to introduce sources of authority, like Alveda King. Alveda is a pro-life activist and niece of the civil rights icon Martin Luther King Jr. She considers Planned Parenthood one of the most racist organizations in our nation's history and abortion the civil rights issue of our time. In a stirring editorial, King recounted how more than 80 percent of Planned Parenthood's abortion facilities are located in inner city neighborhoods, which she believes is an intentional business model. "More African-Americans have died from abortion than from AIDS, accidents, violent crimes, cancer, and heart disease—combined," she explained. "And since 1973 (*Roe v. Wade*), abortion has reduced the black population by more than 25 percent."

For all the Left's preening about "social justice" and "institutional racism," it goes oddly silent when pro-lifers turn the rhetorical tables on Planned Parenthood by asking about the racial—and racist—roots of the pro-abortion movement. Arming your daughter with the truth will give her a boldness of spirit, confident in the knowledge that she is fighting for a just and noble cause.

Parents can also show their daughter how to disentangle the main talking point of the nation's largest abortion provider, that abortions account for only 3 percent of Planned Parenthood's procedures. But this is a classic case of sleight of hand. If a woman receives an ultrasound, pre-abortive counseling, an abortion, and a condom on her way out of a Planned Parenthood facility, then the abortion is recorded as 25 percent of the services provided. In reality, the entire affair was abortion-related.

It's worth noting that all of the additional services that Planned Parenthood offers in the way of women's health can be obtained elsewhere. Mammograms, cancer screenings, pregnancy tests, venereal disease testing, and other services aren't unique. In fact, they are a staple of pro-life pregnancy resource centers, often free of charge.

The bottom line: in its own 2018–2019 annual report, Planned Parenthood admits that its facilities were responsible for 345,672 abortion procedures, but only 4,279 adoption referrals.[8] The numbers don't lie. Planned Parenthood's agenda—and institutional racism—speak loud and clear.

Avoiding Trouble

As the saying goes, the best defense is a strong offense. When it comes to parenting, that means knowing where your girl is and who she's with as much as possible. Parents should know their daughter's friends and the boys she's around. And they cannot be afraid to be restrictive. As my grandmother used to say, "Who are their people, and do they share our values?" Staying on top of your daughter's social life may seem intrusive, but it conditions her choices for when she's old enough to leave home. At that point, parents have little control.

It's no secret that teenagers rebel. Girls might tell their parents that they are going to spend the night at a friend's house while secretly making other plans, such as attending a drinking party. We know because many of us did the same things. But, just as our parents understood, the risks of allowing your child to spend unsupervised time with boys you don't know are not worth it. Girls and boys have different ideas about love, affection, and sexual gratification. That's never going to change. Women tend to fall in love, and they want to please the men they fall in love with. Most young men generally want to enjoy sex and move on. An unwanted pregnancy is a perennial concern, but the risks are heightened in today's hook-up culture. So call ahead. Talk to the parents of your daughter's friend, and make sure everything checks out. Your daughter might get upset; she might roll her eyes. It doesn't matter. Parents must take these kinds of precautions to protect their children.

Talk to your daughter about avoiding trouble. Mature conversations can take many forms. My father told me when I was an adolescent that "there are girls who do, and girls who don't," and he said I had to decide which kind of girl I wanted to be. I knew exactly what he meant. It was never a difficult decision, and church, family, school, and other time-consuming activities certainly helped. Filling your daughter's life with positive influences, knowing the people she's spending time with, and leaving little room for trouble in her day-to-day life is a recipe for success.

Another path is abstinence. It may sound old-fashioned, but abstinence is a surefire way to avoid pregnancy and disease. Teach your daughter to set high standards for herself and her body. Keep close tabs on her beginning around twelve or thirteen years old so that she is used to it when she's sixteen, seventeen, and eighteen.

There is a notion that conservatives are just pro-birth, that we don't care about the child once it's born. Saving a life is a great place to start, but the truth is conservatives are for both—saving the life and helping the mother and baby after it's born.

If your daughter does get pregnant, the conservative response should be unconditional love, not rejection. She will have made a life-changing choice, and the gravity won't be lost on her. Care for her. Exercise forgiveness and grace. It's not the end of the world, but the road ahead will be difficult. Whatever happens, do not allow the situation to be made worse by an abortion. The additional trauma isn't worth it; it's a mistake that lasts forever. There are many options available to support young women and their children. Adoption, family, and other avenues for defending life are plentiful. She will not be alone, and neither will you. Life is too precious, and every challenge—big or small—is an opportunity to live our values.

Defend Life and Celebrate Life with Others

Abortion is morally wrong, and no amount of money or political campaigning is going to change that fact. Conservative parents can help their daughters understand the merits of the issue and prepare them for debates. They can also introduce their daughter to other girls who share the same passion for protecting the unborn. There is tremendous power in communities of like-minded people, and empowerment is just one of many blessings in the conservative pro-life movement.

The largest annual human rights demonstration is the world is the "March for Life" event in Washington, D.C. A sea of women (and men) flood the National Mall in freezing January temperatures to walk down to the U.S. Capitol every year. Unlike the pink hat–wearing feminists who populate the "Women's March," participants aren't protesting anything. They gather to celebrate life. And that includes babies in the womb.

Your daughter could benefit immensely from joining positive, inspiring, and peaceful rallies like the "March for Life." She may also benefit from groups like "Students for Life," a nonprofit organization offering pro-life activities and resources on college campuses around the country. Movie events for films like *Unplanned*, a powerful pro-life feature film, can also carry the message among faith-based and conservative youth groups. Abortion is a horrid practice, but equipping your daughter with pro-life facts and information will empower her to become a voice for the voiceless.

CHAPTER 7

Manage Money Early and Often

If you think the Left isn't interested in shaping the way your daughter thinks about money and economic freedom, think again. Socialism's rising popularity among America's youth didn't happen by accident. Through a highly funded and well-coordinated approach, Leftists have unleashed a seductive socialist economic agenda designed to win over an even greater portion of America's young people. And you might be surprised at the seemingly innocuous places their radical economic messages now show up in your daughter's life.

When most parents hear the name *Teen Vogue*, they imagine a magazine filled with beauty tips, makeup secrets, fashion trends, fitness routines, and perhaps some advice on boys and dating. In reality, *Teen Vogue* has become a radical Leftist publication with a Marxist economic agenda. In November 2020, *Teen Vogue* columnist Kandist Mallett ran an article that declared: "At its core, America's values are white supremacy and capitalism."[1] Mallett explains to teen readers that "from geographic segregation to immigration bans and racist policing, the [United States] has privileged the lives and security of some residents at the expense of others." Furthermore, teen girls are instructed that government redistribution of wealth is the solution to economic inequality. "I don't want to see a 'kinder' capitalism that still forces people to work while they're sick and take on multiple jobs just to get by," declared Mallett. "I want to live in a society that ensures people's basic needs—like housing, food, health care, and a clean environment—by creating programs like universal health care and de-privatization of housing." If you're wondering what she means by "de-privatization of housing," the *Teen Vogue* columnist points to another article where she calls for the end of private property rights and slams the "cruelty of payment-based housing." That article even caught the attention of Texas congressman Dan Crenshaw, who tweeted: "*Teen Vogue* published op-ed that says we should abolish private property rights...along with those pesky police. Just wondering if anyone sees any issues with our next generation reading Marxist propaganda in popular teen magazines?"[2]

I sure do. And I suspect you do as well.

Parents owe it their daughters to teach them about economic freedom, why capitalism produces the best outcomes for the most people, and important financial principles about saving and investing money. Boys typically get the business and money talks while girls get passed over. I urge you to break that tradition. Guiding your daughter will not only help her later in life, it will shape her macroeconomic views. Higher taxes? "No thanks, I work too hard and make too many sacrifices for the government to waste my money." Increase the debt limit? "Absolutely not. We need to pay for what we spend."

Fiscal conservatism is the product of money management lessons learned early in childhood. So let's begin with the basics a young girl should learn to get off to a strong conservative start.

Capitalism vs. Socialism

In 2019, Gallup conducted a major study of young people's attitudes towards capitalism and socialism. The headline from Gallup: "Socialism as Popular as Capitalism among Young Adults in U.S." The survey found that young adults' positive views of capitalism had fallen from 66 percent in 2010 down to just 50 percent—the same as those who viewed socialism positively.[3] This isn't just a failure of our education system; it is a clarion call for parents to actively teach the virtues and values of free-market capitalism and the tyranny of government-controlled economies. As renowned conservative economist Thomas Sowell points out: "Socialism is a wonderful idea. It is only as a reality that it has been disastrous." Sowell is right. But the only way girls will know that is if we teach them.

The simple definition of capitalism is an economic system of voluntary exchange between individuals that produces a mutual benefit. Socialism is marked by government control over the means of production and who benefits. Put simply, capitalism is about freedom; socialism is about government-enforced coercion. Under capitalism, free people are allowed to pursue their own self-interest, take entrepreneurial risks, and win big if they succeed. Under socialism, the government determines winners and losers and seizes and redistributes the wealth workers create. Teaching your daughter that free-market capitalism equals freedom and socialism equals government control is the seed that will bloom a thousand intellectual forests later on.

The father of capitalism, Adam Smith, famously explained this chief tenet in *The Wealth of Nations*: "It is not from the benevolence of the butcher, the brewer[,] or the baker that we expect to eat our dinner, but from their regard to their own interest." What Smith meant is that people pursuing their own self-interest produce greater outcomes for everyone—an "invisible hand" that works to create the most benefit for all. The seller creates jobs and wealth. The buyer receives a product or service. And when more sellers pursue their self-interest and go into business as well, competition drives down the price and products improve. Win-win-win.

Of course, leftists have distorted and abused Smith's concept. They claim capitalism is a system built on greed and sustained by racism that creates the oppression of workers and wealth inequality. Therefore, they claim, the government must step in, seize control, and divide up and redistribute money to ensure "equality of outcomes." These are of course lies, and they further demonstrate liberals' lack of economic understanding, because Adam Smith wrote an entire book called *The Theory of Moral Sentiments* that addressed the moral and legal responsibilities of maintaining free markets. Still, conservatives do not believe in equality of outcomes; we believe in equality of opportunity. How high an individual manages to rise is up to her own efforts, not the decision of government. That's the only way to have a society that distributes wealth fairly.

So how can parents teach these foundational economic principles to their daughters, particularly when they are young? One great way is to start a conversation about how students earn grades in school. It might go something like this: "Let me ask you something. How would you feel if your math teacher told the class that she was going to take that A you earned on your last test and give away part of it to a student who got an F? That way, by averaging your A and his F you both would get a C. Would you be okay with that?" She will say absolutely not. When you ask why, she will likely say, "Because that's not fair. I studied hard and earned my A. The other student did not, which is why he failed the test." And then you ask her the critical follow up question: "Now what would happen on future tests if everyone knew that no matter how hard they study, their grades will be taken from them, averaged together, and everybody receives a C?" And that's the lightbulb moment. "Well, I wouldn't try anymore. No one would. What's the point of working hard if the teacher is just going to steal your grade and give it to someone who didn't try hard?" From there you pivot into a conversation of how that same concept is the difference between capitalism, a system that rewards hard work and sacrifice, versus socialism, one that destroys creativity, seizes property, and redistributes wealth.

Starting with simple conversations like this as early as elementary school can produce enormous benefits for shaping the way your daughter sees the world when it comes to economics—and her place and potential in our economic system. Indeed, teaching young girls about the responsibility and opportunity that comes with earning and managing money is a lot of fun. The key is starting simple when she's young and slowly building from there with practical parenting lessons based on conservative principles.

Attitudes and Communication

Money is *not* the root of all evil. The *love of* or *lust for* money is. That little turn of phrase makes a world of difference, and parents have to be aware of the messages they send when talking about finances in front of their daughter. Saying someone is "filthy rich," for example, implies that there is something inherently dirty or bad about someone who acquires wealth. That view certainly doesn't apply to a person who has earned his or her wealth through hard work, honesty, and innovation. So it's important to examine the language we use when discussing money and wealth with our children. Even seemingly innocent sentiments often carry a secondary message. Parents often express negative money messages in front of their children without realizing it. They may be blowing off steam, and other adults would recognize it as such. But young children are impressionable, and words have consequences, for better or worse. Be careful not to unwittingly corrupt your daughter's ideas about money.

Instead of venting, consciously encourage fiscal optimism. Money is a tool, and managing it wisely provides greater opportunities to help others. Conservatives are also big believers in personal responsibility, so look at the glass as being half full and take steps to improve rather than complain. Instead of beating the "we-can't-afford-it" drum, change your perspective and take initiative. It will help you and your daughter. "How much do your concert tickets cost? Ok, let's make it a goal. We can afford it, just not right now. We have to work and save for the next two months." Teach your daughter that she can have good things; she just has to earn them.

It's also wise for girls to steer clear of people who demonize the rich. The politics of envy and class warfare have gone viral in today's "woke" popular culture. When successful people are derided as the evil "1 percent" who don't pay their "fair share" of taxes, grab your wallet. Top earners pay a very high percentage of all income tax in our "progressive" tax system, and they also create jobs and give to churches and charities. That's something to celebrate in front of your daughter.

Another aspect of communicating about money is to decide how much you want to share with your daughter about family finances. Parents have differing views on this question. Some rarely discuss family financial issues and keep the topic hidden from their kids. Others talk openly about money and bills as if their kids were adults. Girls who grow up in family business environments are often exposed to entrepreneurship and advanced financial conversations at a young age. They tend to develop a certain confidence that comes with managing money. But they shouldn't know too much with respect to numbers.

My view is that parents should discuss family issues in the context of paying for things. The cost of new clothes, for example, involves financial trade-offs. That's helpful for a young girl to understand. The same goes for big-ticket family items like vacations or a new car. You can't have everything just because you want it. Talking about costs means explaining choices. And if parents aren't going to talk about it at home, your daughter will form her ideas about money from somewhere.

Girls don't need to be burdened with financial worries. But talking about money in a way that promotes responsibility is critical. It's healthy for your daughter to know that her braces are expensive, and that mom and dad have worked hard to save for them. Now, she needs to do her part and take care of her teeth, and so on. When your daughter understands hard work and financial stewardship, she's on the right path.

From Piggy Banks to Checking Accounts

Every young child needs a piggy bank. They are an excellent tool for teaching kids about managing money. From pennies to birthday cash, it's fun to watch a girl's eyes light up at the prospect of making another deposit. Take your daughter to the store when she's little and let her pick a piggy bank that she likes. Tell her that saving money is big-girl stuff and watch as she takes pride in her new responsibility.

Another way to drive home the importance of saving when your daughter is young is to fill a glass jar. Every nickel, dime, and dollar goes into a clear glass jar with the promise that she can spend her money once it's full. Toys, ice cream, clothes; the sky is the limit in a child's mind. Taking money out, counting it, and putting it into one-dollar piles will have several immediate benefits. First, your daughter will learn basic math skills. Then comes a sense of proportion: she can buy a Barbie, but not the entire doll house. Finally, she will notice a large empty space in the jar where her money used to be. That's the cost of her toy. She won't just hear the cost; she will *see* it. She can have a full jar or a toy, but she can't have both. Let her decide.

In an age when girls are given so much without an expectation of contributing, this simple exercise is quite valuable. Piggy banks and glass jars don't require a lot of money to be effective, and your daughter never actually spends her money without you. Once the concept of saving is established, it's time to visit a local bank and open a savings account. That's a big day for any kid and a wonderful memory for moms and dads. Have your daughter empty her piggy bank and help pack coin rolls full of pennies, nickels, dimes, and quarters. Establish a joint account, and teach her how to record deposits, withdrawals, and calculate the balance.

As your daughter gets older, a checking account may be in order. I like the idea of starting a girl's checking account at a relatively young age, provided that she has shown financial maturity in earlier exercises. Teach her to keep a checkbook and show her how a deposit or withdrawal will mathematically affect her account balance. A huge part of managing money boils down to math, which even twelve-year-old girls can put into practice. The process is ripe for conversations about how businesses and families must keep positive balances and that politicians and governments tend to make more withdrawals than deposits.

Bank accounts also provide a basis for setting financial goals. Consider sitting down with your daughter and initiating a conversation about what she would like to accomplish. Prompt her with ideas, like saving half of what she makes from this year's babysitting jobs or putting five hundred dollars into her college fund over the next twelve months. When your daughter gets paid, or grandma gives her a Christmas check, she will know exactly where to put it: her bank account. Then she will be ready to learn about creating wealth through investing.

The Wonders of Investing

Albert Einstein once called compound interest the eighth wonder of the world. "He who understands it, earns it...he who doesn't...pays it," he said. Benjamin Franklin said it this way: "Money makes money. And the money that money makes, makes money." Every girl should learn how to make her money work for her, and a modest savings account can even underwrite her first investments. Don't make the mistake of letting early opportunities pass by.

These days, a ten-year-old can understand the stock market. Before the internet, people would have to buy a *Wall Street Journal* and peruse back-page columns of numbers and stock abbreviations to gauge prices and trends. If you wanted to know the price-to-earnings ratio for General Electric, a high market acumen and calculator were needed. Now, websites do all of that in real time. Investing has never been more accessible or easier to understand.

So, pop open a user-friendly stock-price website, such as Google Finance, and show your daughter how stocks work. Explain that green arrows mean gains, and downward red arrows are losses. Watch her interest pique when you tell her that she can literally own a piece of her favorite company. Coca-Cola, Walmart, McDonald's, or whatever floats her boat. Each share of those companies has a price, and your daughter can buy them. She can also follow the stock as it grows or loses value. That's thrilling for many children.

Maybe she's not able or ready to actually purchase a share of stock. That's fine. You can turn it into a fun game. And in fact, an enterprising website called www.stockmarketgame.org has done just that. Let your girl pick a favorite stock and chart its progress over several weeks. Explain as you go. "Mom, Dad, you're not going to believe it! Hershey has gone up twenty five cents!" Then ask her how much money someone would have made had they purchased a hundred shares at the price she started tracking it. Or a thousand shares. Or ten thousand shares. Soon she will visualize the financial possibilities that come through investment. Likewise, if her stock loses money, that's a great opportunity to calculate losses and discuss financial risk. Either way, she's having fun learning basic market and investment principles while gaining the financial confidence she will carry into adulthood.

Delayed Gratification, Opportunity Costs, and Giving

There's a scene in the classic children's movie *Willy Wonka & the Chocolate Factory* where a high-maintenance rich girl named Veruca Salt demands a golden goose from candy magnate Willy Wonka. "Alright Wonka, how much?" her father says, taking out his checkbook. "They're not for sale," he responds. Veruca throws a tantrum and screeches, "I want it now!" It's the perfect depiction of a spoiled brat with no concept of delayed gratification.

This vignette shows life in many families, where parents create tiny tyrants by buying their children things at the drop of a hat. Parents don't always realize when they do this, as it's often easier to pay for something than deal with the fallout of telling a child no. They also want to make their children happy, but taking short cuts doesn't raise them right. Incidentally, Veruca ends up being judged a "bad egg" by a fictitious golden goose machine, and she disappears down a garbage chute. It's a harsh message, but one that's sure to grab a child's attention.

So much of teaching conservative money principles to a daughter is about learning the concept of delayed gratification. It means teaching her that achieving what one desires takes time and hard work. And it also means not making impulsive, foolish choices. Those are valuable lessons that extend far beyond finances. It's about learning that making wise decisions today means she can enjoy the fruits of her labor tomorrow. That's a surefire way to succeed in life. It involves denying an impulse to buy things you can't afford, which is the same principle as your daughter's denying the impulse to sleep at her boyfriend's house or cheat on a test at school. Delayed gratification is essential to both conservatism and good parenting.

Opportunity cost is another important and related conservative concept. Girls learn what it means when they discover that they can't have their cake and eat it too. When it comes to money, girls have to learn to make trade-offs. Mommy and Daddy aren't going to purchase an endless supply of her heart's desires. "Money doesn't grow on trees" is an ageless axiom that helps convey the point. Imagine if our government leaders adhered to it!

Giving your daughter a budget to pay for something she wants will teach her about opportunity cost. Let her decide how to use the resources that she has accumulated from her chores and allowance. She might have to choose between one ideal item or three lesser items. But not everything at once. She'll learn that life is about making choices and that resources are always scarce. That's Economics 101.

Larger purchases can combine delayed gratification and opportunity costs. For example, if your daughter wants a new bicycle, she can work and save to earn it. Help her plan the process. Go online and look at different bikes. How much do they cost? At your daughter's current work and allowance income, how long will it take to save for it? This clarity alone can lead to a good decision. Offer incentives for her to earn more and speed up her savings rate. Remind her that forgoing other spending opportunities will help move her closer to her goal.

Finally, parents need to show that earning money is only valuable insofar as it serves a higher purpose. We don't work just to get richer and richer for the sake of wanton materialism. Rather, we earn money in order to effect change, provide for our family, and help other people. Numerous studies have shown that conservatives give more to charity than liberals. Conservatives believe it's the job of individuals to help others, not government.

Liberals generally want the government to impose social programs and demand higher taxes to pay for them. Conservatives often resist and are portrayed as cruel and selfish. But their outsized giving doesn't square with popular stereotypes. In truth, conservatives want the freedom to give their money where they believe it will be best spent. Religious charities, natural disaster funds, and all manner of private nonprofit organizations are showered with good faith donations every year. The generosity of both working-class and wealthy conservatives knows no bounds. I know that firsthand, as the Clare Boothe Luce Center benefits greatly from compassionate donors who use their resources to help young women learn conservatism.

Individual choice always trumps government coercion. And parental role modeling is critical for teaching girls to give. Show your daughter that it's an important part of life. Include her on your philanthropic decisions where appropriate. Encourage your daughter to dedicate a portion of her earnings to church or charity. Help her choose a path that speaks to her heart. Maybe it's helping children, supporting missionaries, or perhaps families of fallen soldiers. There's no limit to the good your daughter can do, even if her contributions are small. And the greatest lesson of all may just be that giving blesses the giver.

Jobs Are the Key

Most conservative women whom I have met share a common experience: they had jobs when they were young. It's not a coincidence. I have asked many interns what they would do to raise a conservative girl. The answers varied, but the top response was always a job. Why? Because a job develops work ethic, personal responsibility, problem solving, accountability, and financial knowledge at an early age.

By having a job, girls learn to work for money. An employer isn't a parent. An employer doesn't give money away; a girl has to earn it. Girls also realize how much they have to work to be able to buy the things they want. And if they want more, they have to work harder and smarter, and likely more hours. Then, when taxes eat a chunk of their wages, reality hits home, and they wonder what in the world the government is doing with their hard-earned cash. When your daughter brings home her paycheck, talk to her about the Social Security tax. Ask her what she thinks about paying her hard-earned money into a program that's teetering on bankruptcy and unlikely to meet its future obligations—money she won't see for fifty years or more.

Parents can talk about financial responsibility, but a job makes those lessons a part of her lived experience. Not everyone agrees that girls should work in high school or college. Studies should always come first, and higher college admission standards may involve extra preparation. Public service requirements can also take up time that may have been traditionally available for part-time employment. But, generally, girls should still work. They can limit their hours, but the benefits go way beyond the drawbacks. This had always been accepted wisdom until relatively recently.

Teenage employment has plummeted since the millennial generation. In 1989, nearly 60 percent of 16- to 19-year-olds had summer jobs. 44 percent worked year-round. Today, about a third of teenagers have summer jobs, and fewer than 30 percent work the rest of the year. Kids are missing out on so many of the lessons that helped make America an economic powerhouse. And it's not just about earning and saving money, as important as that is. It's writing a résumé, preparing for a job interview, talking to adults, learning new skills, being accountable, and developing future references. That's what I look for when young ladies apply to be summer fellows.

A job also forces girls to go outside their social bubbles and to work with different types of people. Scooping ice cream and making pizzas forces a girl to interact with people of different demographic backgrounds. Keeping hours, working with others, going to work when others are idle—these are crucial to her character development. You never know what your daughter will learn. Working a cash register will teach math and money skills. Sadly, many of today's teens don't know how to count change for a cash purchase. Maybe she will think of better ways to contribute and move up the company ladder. Maybe she'll recoil at manual labor and rededicate herself to her studies so that stocking supermarket shelves won't be her future career, just as my son did. Nothing his father or I could have told him could have motivated him more.

That said, parents do need to exercise discretion about where their daughter works. Anything that risks her safety should be out of the question. Restaurants that serve alcohol and release their wait staff late at night can be problematic. Likewise, jobs that require girls to wear skimpy uniforms or are in dangerous parts of town are asking for trouble. There are plenty of employment opportunities without those risks.

Student Loan Debt

Often, preparations for college start as early as middle school, with "tiger moms" and motivated parents steering their children toward academic paths and extracurricular activities that will sparkle on admissions applications. Tutors who specialize in entrance exams are busier than ever. But paying for school is often a secondary concern that ends up leaving many young adults and families buried beneath mountains of debt. It doesn't have to be that way.

Just as talking about college can help your daughter envision life after high school, talking about paying for it can help her avoid the student loan–debt trap. There are different approaches. One involves sitting your daughter down early in high school and asking her how she is going to pay for college. Put the onus on her, and let her mental wheels start turning. "You mean, you aren't going to take care of it, Mom?" Explain that the goal is to reduce debt and keep student loans off the table or held to a minimum. Panic may or may not ensue, but her thought process will shift from, "I'll take out huge loans like everyone else if Mom and Dad don't pay," to, "I'd better figure out how this is going to work." After the initial shock, initiate conversations about earning, saving, scholarships, and trade-offs. Perhaps encourage her to stay closer to home and attend her first two years at a community college or a state school rather than maxing out her most expensive options.

Today, students are racking up debt and avoiding hard choices because they tell themselves that college should be free and that the government will eventually pick up the tab. They run up big tabs in the hopes that politicians will cancel their student loan debt. Senators Bernie Sanders and Elizabeth Warren popularized student loan bailouts as part of their recent efforts to win votes, and many liberals think it's only a matter of time before the Democrats take up their cause. For the record, there are currently $1.6 trillion in student debt. Wiping the slate clean rewards debtors while punishing those who made financial sacrifices and honored their loan commitments. Those who were unable to attend college would get the short end of the stick, as the policy would transfer wealth from their paychecks to college graduates.

Debt is tricky for conservatives. We want to avoid it, but sometimes it's necessary. I was determined to avoid student loans in college. It took hard work and tough choices. I had to take a year off between my junior and senior undergraduate years. Living at home, I worked at a bank to save money and took classes at night at nearby colleges for half of my senior year. It wasn't fun, but that's what I needed to do. Nobody was going to bail me out, and I was better for it. Years later, I went to four years of law school at night and paid my way through. I took a small loan my fourth year, which was my husband's first year of night law school. It's possible to still do that today if your daughter is willing to sacrifice.

Make it a goal to sidestep student loan debt as much as possible. Help your daughter earn scholarships, grants, and other available financial assistance opportunities. Even parents who can afford to pay for college with one stroke of a pen can raise their daughter to appreciate the costs of her education. Providing the basics and letting your daughter work for the rest can help her build self-reliance, rather than nurture dependence.

Beating the Credit Card Game

Credit cards are one of the earliest financial temptations your daughter will face. Shiny advertisements and online pop-up ads are everywhere. Many young women ignore credit cards in the beginning. They have no experience and are unsure about them. Then, they start thinking, "Hmm, I can't afford what I want, but I could just charge it and pay later. That's what adults do, right?"

Sadly, that's often true. But it's a dangerous thought for young people to indulge. Without parental oversight, girls can get into a mess. In a worst-case scenario, they max out one card, then take out another. Soon they are flipping through their wallets to find a card that still has room. When girls make these sorts of choices, they run the risk of not only ruining their own financial future, but of ruining that of their family as well. Teach your daughter about the credit card debt spiral, where making minimum payments will keep her indebted even if she feels like she's staying on top of things. Paying the full balance off every month is key.

One way for parents to deal with credit cards is to forbid them. There can be no disaster if there's no card to begin with. None of my children were allowed to have credit cards—except for use in emergencies. I'm not knocking that approach, but your daughter is going to leave your house one day and make her own decisions. Moreover, building a strong credit rating may be vital to her future financial well-being. So, you could help her learn about responsible credit card practices under your supervision rather than leaving her to go at it alone.

Start by teaching her that credit cards are a neutral financial tool. They aren't inherently good or bad but can be either depending on how they're used. Treating them mistakenly as a modern-day cash can have many hidden costs. They also have practical uses beyond helping establish one's credit rating. For example, it's much safer for girls to carry a card in case of emergency than keeping a wad of cash stuffed in her purse.

Parents can help by sorting through card offers with their daughter and finding a good fit for her needs. Parents can put the card in their name or, if your daughter is eighteen, her name. Banks don't typically lend to eighteen-year-olds with no employment or credit history, so parents will likely need to be involved, unless the card comes with highly unfavorable terms to offset risk. That's obviously something to avoid. Take the time to explain how interest rates work, minimum payments, and the importance of beating the bank by paying off expenses before the end of the month. Help her identify hidden fees and understand that fancy bonus offers are designed to entice large expenditures.

If you get a credit card for your daughter or if she qualifies on her own, consider lowering the limit. This is a great way to bypass potential damage from impulsive decisions while maintaining the benefits. If the card comes with a five thousand dollar limit, contact the lender and lower it to five hundred dollars. This would provide the ability to pay for food and cell phone bills when your daughter is away at school while maintaining an emergency resource if she breaks down on the interstate, for example. It's also a manageable amount to pay off should she fall behind.

Late high school or early college is a good time to have them read Dave Ramsey, Suze Orman, or Sam Edelman—authors who give sound financial advice with some differing points of view. There are also several personal financial apps that are helpful for young people to use to manage their money online. Learning the keys to financial management when she's young can save your daughter considerable headache later in life.

Credit cards come down to personal responsibility, which is a core conservative trait. Teach your daughter the right way to manage credit and help her build financial confidence. And if she gets into trouble, do not bail her out. Give her the gift of learning from her mistakes.

Entrepreneurship

Entrepreneurship teaches girls that they can be more than just employees. They can start a business or innovate their way to new heights. It takes identifying an opportunity, taking a risk, and working for profit. It can be as simple as opening a lemonade stand in your neighborhood or selling items on eBay.

Parents can show their daughter successful small businesses and explain how the different parts—like product development, marketing, and customer service—make the whole thing work; a job is just one aspect of a business. Sharing stories of how corporate giants started from an idea and lots of hard work can also feed your daughter's imagination. *Shark Tank* entrepreneur Lori Greiner, for example, built her empire from a plastic earring organizer that helped women keep track of their jewelry. Why not plant those seeds for your daughter?

Not everyone is cut out to be an entrepreneur. Your daughter doesn't have to be. The point is that entrepreneurship helps girls see the big picture. They learn that the harder they work and the more creative they become at finding solutions to problems, the "luckier" they will be. It also teaches the value and dedication of job creators. It's difficult to become a socialist when parents help their daughters develop an affinity for creating jobs and opportunity through hard work early on.

Putting It All Together

Teaching girls the principles of economic freedom, capitalism, and responsible money management has tremendous benefits for the rest of their lives. It engenders fiscal responsibility, empowers them to stand on their own two feet, and weaves delayed gratification into their worldview.

Parents can play a pivotal role in their daughter's development by helping her save early in childhood. Piggy banks and savings accounts go a long way toward building this initial habit. As she matures, parents can shift to helping her balance a checkbook, invest in the stock market, and get entrepreneurial ideas off the ground. Conversations about student loans while girls start high school can lay the groundwork for reducing debt after college. And if you allow them to have credit cards, providing supervision, advice, apps, and book suggestions will help them make healthy spending decisions.

Girls are more than capable of learning about the power of capitalism and how to manage money. Give your daughter the gift of the confidence that comes through managing money early and often.

CHAPTER 8

Service to Others Yields Self-Reliance

President Reagan once brought up the parable of the Good Samaritan during an Oval Office meeting with his chief political strategist and pollster, Dick Wirthlin. "You know," Reagan said, "it is often overlooked that the person who *really* gained the most was the Good Samaritan who rendered service, not the person who received it. I think the real lesson of the parable is that we benefit most when we help a neighbor in need." As Wirthlin recounts, in President Reagan's eyes, "America didn't owe him thanks. He owed America thanks for giving him the chance to serve."[1]

Reagan understood that something special happens when we serve others. An outer benefit is given and an inner blessing received. Those who receive are able to stand taller knowing that people care. Their needs are met through kindness, and gratitude often fills their hearts. The giver is also blessed in a way that transcends the hustle and bustle of everyday life. You can't quantify it; the world just becomes a better place. And when your daughter gives with a pure heart, she will know a deep, inner satisfaction. She will become more of who she was made to be.

When we give, we grow. There's less need for government and dependence when we volunteer. Service changes lives—I've seen it many times with my own eyes—and parents can help their daughter experience the joy that comes from giving no matter how small her contribution. I recommend she always start with people in your own family who are in need. If you can't be kind to your relatives, it is hard to make up for it elsewhere. Scripture warns us not to turn our back on our own! *Is it not to share your food with the hungry and to provide the poor wanderer with shelter—when you see the naked, to clothe them, and not to turn away from your own flesh and blood?* (Isaiah 58:7).

In addition to the parable of the Good Samaritan there is also a story in the Gospels called the Widow's Mite. A poor woman quietly gives only a couple of pennies to the Temple treasury, and yet her gift has more impact than the large sums of wealth given by those seeking public recognition. The woman gave willingly with no expectation of credit or praise. Instead, she offered all she had with pure intentions. It's a powerful lesson that's still relevant today.

Still, relaying the concept of giving, receiving, and self-reliance to girls can be tricky. We live in a "what's-in-it-for-me" culture where volunteering time and energy for unpaid work is counterintuitive. As a rule, young people tend to shy away from initiating selfless service work, especially outside of religious contexts. If they don't understand that it's truly better to give than to receive, then service is just one more expectation added to their already crowded plate. It sounds like mandatory virtue signaling to teenage ears.

Parents can push their daughter to volunteer, but the magic doesn't come from obligation. It comes from a sincere desire to help other people. Consider your daughter's "mite." What are her passions? What does she care about to the extent that she will want to give? How can she make a difference in that space? Before exploring ways to motivate your daughter, it's important to understand the folly of forced service—a weak substitute for the real thing.

Forced Service Misses the Mark

There is a big difference between choosing to do something and being forced to do it. If your daughter had to serve food at a lunch counter or pick up trash on the side of the road because someone forced her, it may look the same on the outside as the person who volunteers to do it, but it's not. One side seeks out the opportunity to serve. They are self-motivated, willing participants. They want to be there. The other side is doing what they have to do. They are more apt to go through the motions and get it over with, while harboring potential resentments. Something inside is missing.

The military draft is a good example of the difference. Young men were forced to join the military during the Vietnam War. They had to serve or pull strings to get out of it. Rather than amass the biggest motivated fighting force possible, the draft undermined the authenticity of service, and the result was an inferior system to what we have today. Anyone who wears the uniform deserves great respect. God bless them. But I come from a military family, and I can tell you that most service members are totally opposed to forcing people to serve, except in the most extreme circumstances. They would rather have one volunteer who wanted to enlist than ten people who were forced to comply. Why? Because you can't make people want something. Forcing them produces weaker morale and results than service born from free choice.

Yet our education system imposes mandatory service on many children these days. Like so many misguided initiatives, the intentions seem good, but the unintended consequences are predictable. Students have to log public service hours, or they can't graduate. Sometimes it's a requirement for scholarships, college admissions, or, in the case of one Clare Boothe Luce Center summer fellow, to join the National Honor Society. It doesn't make sense. Helping others is wonderful. But the idea of mandatory volunteerism is an oxymoron that helps nobody.

Studies have shown that mandatory volunteer service undermines the desire to volunteer in the future.[2] Please don't misunderstand; there are good things that can come from these programs. But ultimately they do not work. The inside change isn't there. Something important is missing.

I spoke with a group of summer fellows about the issue, and their answers were surprising. Initially, only one young woman said that mandatory service defeated the purpose of giving. All service was good service, the rest assumed. But they had never really thought about it. That's when I realized the discussion was perfect for parents to have with their daughters. Compulsion and choice are two very different motivations that lead to opposing outcomes.

The more we talked, the more these bright young women understood that genuine service is motivated by an internal conviction that makes people more self-reliant. You don't need government-run schools to make you serve—or hoity-toity private school administrators for that matter. Government programs and oxymoronic mandates crowd out self-initiative and foster a shallow concept of giving. If you want to encourage charity, it has to be voluntary. One of the girls hit the nail on the head: "Requiring service hours doesn't energize the grace we have inside us." I asked her what she meant, knowing she was absolutely right. "The virtue that grows inside of us; that can't be mandated," she replied. Exactly.

Making people give also has the effect of turning them away from what they are supposed to be gaining. Girls may be forced to perform community service as a condition of academic approval even if it's at the expense of real needs at home. Caring for a disabled sibling or an aging grandmother with Alzheimer's disease doesn't count. But checking boxes on forms so that school administrations can advertise their moral superiority does count. It's about doing what you are told rather than what's right for your family. Why not reward genuine service if it's outside the parameters of a school program?

There's also the problem of over-scheduling. Many girls are maxed out with studies, activities, jobs, family responsibilities, and social pressures. Adding unpaid make-work to the mix is unfair. It can increase anxiety and detract time from your daughter's priorities, including her self-initiated service commitments.

Some students cheat to get out of their required hours, while others never fully commit to any cause. You can't dictate someone's inner life or mandate kindness and compassion. You can only force people to comply with directives. That's why compulsion is essential for socialism and left-wing philosophy, and the freedom to choose is a conservative value. There are definitely people on the Left who use mandatory community service programs to impose their views, and they want to train your daughter to change society in a leftward direction.

Of course, we want to encourage young people to give, be virtuous, and to step outside of themselves. And some people may somehow benefit from forced service. But parents need to understand that it misses the mark and gives a false impression of what genuine service is all about. Do not let government schools—or private schools, which aren't much better when it comes to imposing views—raise your daughter. Families must make their own choices, and parents should shepherd their daughter away from compulsory programs and toward real service opportunities.

Virtue Signaling

Before moving to more positive aspects of service, parents should recognize the phenomenon of virtue signaling and how its adherents can put conservative girls in the crosshairs of social activists. Put simply, virtue signaling is when people publicly express their high moral character, but without authenticity. It's a fake service-mentality that tends to coincide with attacking people who disagree. "Look at me! I am a good person because I support woke social activism. If you don't agree with my opinions, then you are a racist, homophobic woman-hater!"

Such unseemly behavior is part of the "Cancel Culture" that's rampant on college campuses and social media. It has also infected elements of the news media and our political discourse. This new moralism is a cheap veneer of compassion that covers a desperate need for approval and attention. Something inside is missing. Shallow nods to serving others doesn't fill the void. It's self-promotion without actual sacrifice. Anyone can bandwagon this week's feel-good trending hashtag on Facebook or Twitter, but who is going to put in the real work to help others with a selfless, joyful heart? You are much more likely to find girls in churches and synagogues helping poor children and the elderly than campus radicals who aggressively push politics from behind a keyboard.

Do not let your daughter be dissuaded from the real thing. Teach her that service is quiet, not self-promoting. The idea of anonymous giving is a great way to check her motivations. Is your daughter giving so she can brag and gain something for herself, or is she serving others regardless of whether anyone outside her circle knows about it?

Virtue signaling is the polar opposite of anonymous giving, and it's become a cultural force. Corporations, media, athletes, celebrities, and politicians are increasingly prone to shaping their brands around pseudo-service. Many give money and attention to groups and causes that intentionally use the thin outward appearance of service to advance radical political goals. It's a way of promoting themselves while keeping the mob at bay. Claiming to support the Black Lives Matter organization on Instagram, participating in campus protests against Israel, or jumping into an online mob to get a random person fired from their job or thrown out of school simply because they ran afoul of activist social priorities does nothing to help people in need.

Your daughter does not have to follow the crowd. She can embrace the idea of equal opportunity without becoming a follower of the Marxist-inspired group receiving hundreds of millions of dollars to affect political outcomes. Selflessly volunteering to help underprivileged children learn to read or giving up some free time to help a children's cancer ward at a local hospital is infinitely more valuable to humanity than wearing T-shirts with glib political phrases or tweeting how great you are.

Instilling the Willingness to Serve

If making people volunteer fails the internal change test, or is used to advance an agenda, then how can conservative parents raise their daughter to want to volunteer? You can't force a choice; it has to come organically. But let's be real: most kids don't wake up on a Saturday morning itching to visit a retirement home or spend their spare time making care packages for soldiers serving overseas during the holidays. They know it's a good idea, but that doesn't make service a priority.

Families with religious backgrounds have it easier. Churches and synagogues are constantly engaged in voluntary service projects. Helping the poor, easing the struggles of sick and hurting souls, staffing a pregnancy center, and blessing people without payment or expectation of reward is a major aspect of faith. The Bible makes hundreds of exhortations to give, and the benefits of putting others before oneself have been known for millennia. The key then is making giving and service fun.

One excellent family service activity is Operation Christmas Child.[3] This is a charity run by Reverend Franklin Graham's Samaritan's Purse that allows kids and parents to pack a shoebox filled with toys and essential items that is then shipped across the world to children in need. Girls of any age can help go to the store and pick out special items to pack in their gift boxes or build one online. There's even a way to track your girl's gift box to see where it ends up. It's a fun, simple, low-cost way to experience the joy that comes through serving others and sharing God's love. Conservative Chuck Colson's Prison Fellowship offers a similar service activity called Angel Tree that delivers Christmas gifts to children whose parents are incarcerated, as well as a Bible to Angel Tree parents.[4] And, of course, since 1947, the United States Marine Corps Toys for Tots program has given kids and families an opportunity to collect gifts for needy children, resulting in an amazing 584 million toys distributed and 265 million children supported.[5] With so many wonderful groups and organizations to choose from, your daughter will have plenty of ways to get involved with your help.

As with any teaching, the best way to influence your daughter is to demonstrate the qualities you wish to see in her. If you want your daughter to work hard, demonstrate your work ethic. If you want her to serve, then volunteer. Parents have credibility when they lead by example, and girls absorb what they see in their families. Actions don't just speak louder than words; they speak thousands of times louder.

Parents, like CEOs, drill instructors, or anyone else in a leadership position, must practice what they preach if they want to effect change in those they lead. There are never any guarantees, but your daughter is much more likely to develop a sincere desire to serve if she sees her mom and dad engaged in the wonders of giving. It doesn't have to be a huge sacrifice, either. Service can be performed within a family, for example. It can involve helping a neighbor or child of an alcoholic mother or absent father. It can also involve fundraising, foreign service, or building an organization. It's up to you, but the principles are the same at every level.

Start within your own family. Commit random acts of selflessness at home, and don't make a big fuss about it. Do kind things without looking for applause and gain; your daughter will notice. Then, reach beyond the four walls of your home and help people you don't know. Don't expect anything in return, and persist through the inevitable hiccups. Once you have experienced the joy that comes from an impoverished child's smile or the satisfaction from knowing you contributed to the genuine well-being of others, invite your daughter into the experience. Show her how it's done.

Parents can also help align their daughter's passions with genuine service commitments. The problem of mandatory service programs is that they dictate what girls are allowed to do or they provide a shortlist of approved items. In other words, your daughter has very little say in how she can dedicate herself to others. Identify what pulls your daughter's heartstrings and introduce volunteer opportunities so she can make a difference.

Putting flags or wreaths on veterans' graves is an incredibly meaningful service opportunity, especially if there are any veterans or service members in your family. Helping an elderly neighbor with yardwork or even shoveling his or her sidewalk when it snows is a special way for her to bless someone she knows with her service. Volunteering to pick up groceries, put up Christmas trees, and holiday decorations are also kind ways to offer helpful service to the elderly, single parents, or someone who is sick or recovering from surgery.

If your daughter loves animals, why not ask her to volunteer at an animal shelter? She could dedicate her love and affection for animals while feeling the deep gratification that comes from serving them. She will connect to something outside of herself and receive blessings that outweigh material reward. If she has fond memories of the beach, help her organize a trash pick-up at different beaches in your area. If she has experienced losing a loved one to breast cancer, have her work with breast cancer patients in need. The spark of life that comes from giving and receiving can be ignited when your daughter finds meaning in how she spends her time. And the growth that comes from touching lives far surpasses look-at-me liberal do-gooding.

Church missions and self-initiated commitments that align with your daughter's personal sympathies will naturally motivate her to help others. She will want to serve and will develop self-reliance as a result. Parents should look at their daughter as the individual that she is and consider her passions, abilities, confidence—with common sense when it comes to safety—and encourage her to do things that fit.

Another way of motivating your daughter is to frame service around solving a problem. What does she care about? Tell her it's time to stop thinking that someone else will deal with it and to get in the game. If the problem is poverty, she can help. Don't assume the government is handling it. Conservatives believe that employment is preferable to welfare. So, a potential solution could be calling businesses and contacting strangers to ask for spare office-appropriate clothes so that low-income people can present well at job interviews. If the problem is abortion, perhaps she can volunteer at a pregnancy center. Maybe she answers phones or rounds up baby clothes for single moms. She could volunteer to help at the annual March for Life or organize a group of friends and family to attend with her. Just a few hours here or there can help a lot of people.

Finally, teaching your daughter that service is a privilege—not a chore—can help develop a sincere impulse to serve others. It's an inversion of how most people think of volunteerism, but it works. One of the many benefits of belonging to a community of faith is that giving is embedded into a worldview. It's not a foreign concept that has to be mandated; it's part of the fabric of living. Mission trips, for example, are commonplace. They are awesome opportunities. Girls travel to places like South America or Africa with a supervised group, make new friends with shared values, and help people in need. There is nothing wrong with trips to different parts of America, either.

Rather than make your daughter go on an overseas mission or push her to join a similar secular trip, treat them like an amazing privilege. They are certainly more meaningful than drinking margaritas for a week on a senior class trip to Cancún. Teach your daughter that service can be an adventure with lifelong memories that produce lasting fulfillment. And if you want to go a step further, make her earn it. Service trips cost money, and even though parents may want to pay for them because it's a wonderful thing, encourage your daughter to earn part of her own way. This reinforces the idea of lived values.

Making service a privilege doesn't have to be a grand opportunity. It can also look like taking your daughter grocery shopping for a local can drive or dropping off donations. If she's had good behavior, then she can go with mom on her service errands. If not, she may miss out. One of the blessings of volunteering is the people you meet along the way. Children are particularly impressionable when it comes to meeting adults in these contexts, and not being able to see Mr. or Mrs. so-and-so or pet the animals at the dog shelter can carry a certain currency with kids. This approach works especially well with little girls. Making service fun when they are young helps shape their volunteer spirit as they grow older.

The Many Benefits of Serving Others

There are so many benefits to serving others that it's hard to know where to begin. That said, authentic service isn't performed for personal benefit. It's a selfless act made on behalf of other people. The beauty, however, is that when your daughter gives irrespective of reward, wonderful blessings will flow to her anyway. Genuine service is like a boomerang—it always comes back to the giver.

Happiness. Satisfaction. Joy. Love. These are among the most precious gifts in life, and they come seamlessly when we give with pure intentions. Parents who have experienced the joy that comes from selflessness can share the message with their daughter. Paint the picture. Let her know about life's treasures that are worth more than gold. Help her experience the warmth that comes from overwhelming gratitude when you are able make a difference in someone's life. If parents aren't familiar with this joy, start volunteering ASAP—and take your daughter with you!

Giving also increases confidence and counteracts the stress that comes from dwelling on one's own problems. In other words, if your daughter wants self-esteem, then she should do things that earn her respect and commendation. Service further provides a sense of purpose. There's nothing more effective at getting out of your own head than helping another person. That's what 12-Step groups like Alcoholics Anonymous are based on. You help others to help yourself, and things get better. It's common sense, but scientific studies also confirm it. Research shows that giving feels good and can even increase health outcomes in people with chronic illnesses.

Of course, there are many practical benefits to service, as well. Commitments often involve learning new skills and extensive training. Those skills may be transferable to future job opportunities and taught to others again and again. It's also easier to get a foot in the door in an area your daughter cares about if she is willing to volunteer instead of looking to get paid. If she wants to be a doctor, volunteering to serve hospital patients is a great way to start down that path. Increased social skills, new contacts and friends, face-to-face interactions with people outside of her bubble, and a greater ability to get things done all come from saying yes to serving others or a cause your daughter cares about.

Parents can watch their daughter become more self-reliant as she grows through giving. Her sincere efforts will also support self-reliance in her community or wherever she dedicates herself. When you serve others through voluntary means, it reduces the need for government in that space. Witnessing the difference between government dependency and voluntary service will inform your daughter's conservative views in ways that textbooks and news articles never will. She will see the difference between choice and compulsion and service versus dependency first-hand.

The Bigger Picture

The libertarian author Ayn Rand once wrote a collection of essays that were compiled into a book called *The Virtue of Selfishness*. The writings expound her Objectivism, which considers altruism a destructive force and selfishness the guiding principle for progress. It's a stark reminder that rigid libertarians are not conservatives, though we have plenty of overlap. Parents should impress upon their daughter that service is not a function of economic value and that there is much more to life than supply, demand, price, and efficiency. There are smiles, children, love, and humanity. Giving with pure intentions isn't wasteful; it's wonderful.

Ask you daughter, what would happen if everyone decided not to serve? Consider the left-wing assault on police or the harmful view that America's military is a tool of oppression. What if cops and soldiers stopped showing up? Think about the firefighters who risk their lives to save others from grave danger, or the selfless inner-city Catholic school teachers that stay late to make sure that a struggling child learns the basics of reading and math. If these folks quit, our society fails. Thankfully, we will always have a class of people who will step up and sacrifice for the rest of us. They should be celebrated and their contributions honored.

Sadly, the culture seems to be going in the opposite direction, with spoiled multi-millionaire athletes kneeling during the national anthem, celebrities badmouthing their own country for cheap applause, and corporate giants feeding the politics of envy all the way to the bank. All of this takes America's servants for granted, those who keep our streets safe, and the private volunteers who help those in need. Parents must teach their daughters to recognize the big picture—those who serve in our communities and at the national level are doing meaningful work.

As individuals, we benefit greatly from choosing to help others. As citizens of this great land, we have a civic duty to make it a better place, free of dependency, government intrusion, and political abuse. It's a duty that can be willingly embraced, and parents can help instill this impulse in their daughter.

Fly the American flag. Take pride in the good, and praise the sacrifices of those who have given so much for the rest of us to live in peace and prosperity. Teach your daughter to put her little right hand over her heart when she says the Pledge of Allegiance or when she hears the first notes of the "Star-Spangled Banner." Teach her history so that she will know when she's being led astray, and take her with you to vote. These actions honor the service of patriots and show girls that we have much to be grateful for—and that it's only right that we should choose to give back.

At a Glance

When your daughter gives, she will receive. She will grow and become more of who she was created to be. She will gain self-reliance, and she will influence people through her honest intentions and hard work. It may be difficult and thankless at times, but the rewards are worth it. Humility. Gratitude. Joy. Happiness. You can't buy those things, but they come freely when you give. Chasing goals, earning degrees, and making money are admirable. But giving and serving is what life is really all about, and it makes all of us better.

Authentic service cannot be forced; it comes from making a sincere choice to help others. Teach your daughter the magic of service, starting with those in need in your own family. Teach her that it feels wonderful to help someone in need or advance a cause that brings good into the world even though, and in fact because, she is giving her time and energy away for free. Parents can start by volunteering themselves and experiencing the joy that comes from giving in the presence of their daughter. Consider bringing her along. Help her identify her passions and how she can engage them through service commitments. Then, watch as she blossoms.

CHAPTER 9

Campus Activism Isn't Just for Feminists

When parents raise their daughter to be conservative, they instill a healthy approach to life. Girls become stronger, freer, and more self-reliant. They thrive knowing who they are, where they come from, and what matters. But to what effect? It's perfectly fine for a young woman to keep her beliefs to herself once she's matured past the rigors and rules of childhood. Sharing the message, however, will create the change America so badly needs.

The stakes are high. The Left is well-funded and well-organized. It's also small in number but manages to dominate the culture. Ground zero is the university system. In many ways, it serves as an indoctrination incubator for wave upon wave of activists who graduate and move into media, government, education, law, and other influential institutions. We cannot afford to cede territory on college campuses anymore.

The good news is that we can fight—with grace and integrity. Conservative girls can be activists too. Your daughter doesn't have to morph into a screeching, man-hating, America-hating banshee to get her point across. She doesn't have to adopt the tactics of radical feminism to combat radical feminists. That's not what conservatives do. We adhere to principles. We revere the Constitution that limits the power of government, salute the flag, and obey the rule of law. We learn our arguments and we stand up for our beliefs. We win by remaining true to ourselves and by changing hearts and minds, not by rioting, intimidating, and silencing those who disagree.

Parents can rest assured that there are plenty of people and organizations ready to support their daughter on her journey from student to student-activist and beyond. There is safety in numbers, and exponential growth in campus communities with shared values. Joining a conservative group and realizing that I could effect positive change are what sparked my activism many years ago. It's also what prompted the founding of the Clare Boothe Luce Center for Conservative Women. There are a number of wonderful conservative-leaning colleges you may want to consider for your daughter.

My third son went to Hillsdale College in Michigan, while my other two boys went to colleges in Ohio, New York, and Washington, D.C. If I had to do it over again, I would say to them all in their senior year of high school, "You can go to Hillsdale, or you can go to work." It is that much better—academically and socially.

A few of the other good conservative-friendly colleges I would recommend include Grove City College, College of the Ozarks, Liberty University, and Franciscan University of Steubenville. Many schools like Notre Dame and William and Mary have a reputation for being conservative, but they are not. I know too many conservative-activist students who have been condemned, harassed, and shut down at these and other similar schools.

Some parents may think it is more prestigious for their daughter to attend a well-known school. And who knows, conservative parents and family may be proud that their daughter was admitted to Wellesley or Smith College. But they may also spend the rest of their life ruing the day she became a Wellesley liberal like Hillary Clinton, who started college as a conservative Goldwater girl.

The truth is that if those prestigious schools were doing their jobs in educating our daughters well, this book wouldn't have to be written.

Prestigious schools have failed us, but most people are in denial about what happens to their daughters at those schools. These schools have transformed our country in a way that is not desirable. In the years these schools have been expanded and lavishly funded, our daughters have had more abortions, more failed marriages, and more self-doubt. Instead of strong, confident women, suddenly we have way too many whiners. I have not been impressed by any of the schools that emphasize race, class, and gender in admissions, hiring faculty and staff, housing, and other school processes. Young people are more favorable to socialism because colleges refuse to teach the disastrous side of Marxism. You won't understand the freedom philosophy if you don't read Friedman, Hayek, Laffer, and Walter Williams. And the students who are obsessed with race have never read or heard the ideas of Thomas Sowell or Charles Murray. There is just no substitute for reading freedom-oriented literature, and they clearly don't get the well-rounded education that fully informs them in this way at most colleges. I do know a few girls who make it through the prestigious Ivies with their conservatism intact. They are among the best and strongest of our conservative women leaders. But far more go the way of Hillary Clinton.

I would be more likely to hire a young woman who graduated from Hillsdale for my staff than a Duke graduate. The conservative-leaning colleges are a better choice for your daughter and will give her a high-quality path for her future. Many students I know have found life-long mentors at these schools, professors they call on over and over again throughout their lives for help and advice.

All of the lessons discussed thus far add up to a developed sense of personal values. The next step is for your daughter to put them into action and to get out there and advance what she believes. That can look many different ways. There will be times when raising a hand in class to offer a dissenting point of view will be a courageous decision. Perhaps your daughter will run for student government or assert her principles in a debate setting. Maybe she will bring a conservative speaker to campus and cause a stir. She may have to pick and choose her battles. But standing up at the right time is what activism and leadership are all about. That's how change is created. After all, what's the point of having values if you hide them when they are needed most?

Another Brief Story

I was viciously attacked for my beliefs for the first time in 1972. Radical feminism was ascendant, and America's "Cultural Revolution" was in full swing. The experience is seared into my memory. I was a senior at Briarcliff College in Briarcliff Manor, New York. Senator George McGovern was challenging President Richard Nixon in an upcoming presidential election, and I had decided to get involved. I had spent the previous year studying abroad at the University of London and had seen socialism up close. I recognized similar themes in the McGovern campaign and was determined to make a difference—not that I was a Nixon fan.

I formed a Young Americans for Freedom chapter at school and participated in a "Youth against McGovern" effort. I invited students to hear a YAF speaker against McGovern, and I made a flyer with McGovern's picture that included some controversial quotes, then passed them out and put them in mailboxes. It was nothing "Youth against Nixon" wasn't doing. Walking down the hall one day, a sociology professor approached me out of nowhere. She was furious. She backed me into a corner and began berating me. "How dare you!" she yelled. "How could you say these things about George McGovern? Why would you make a flyer?" I was shocked into silence. She had assumed the worst about me, as if my views were illegitimate and I had no right to express them.

Students were passing by and stopped to witness the commotion. It was embarrassing. She was outraged. I struggled to find my voice, but she wouldn't let me speak. People were listening and looking; it was awful. I can still see her triggered expression when she stormed away in anger as I started to speak. I was just starting to think that I could be a leader, that I could speak up for conservative ideas, and an adult who was supposed to further my development wanted to stifle it. That confrontation presented me with a choice: either I would stand up, share my beliefs, and defend myself, or I would melt from the embarrassment and hide. I still remember that moment vividly all these years later.

You can probably guess my decision. I was raised to work hard and "get in there and fight." So that's what I did. I did what I thought was right; I got attacked for it, and even though it was unfair and hurtful, I got over it and grew emboldened. Nearly fifty years later, that event continues to motivate me. There's gold on the other side of the dragon. Campus bullies can't win if your daughter shares her beliefs and continues the good fight. Always remember that.

Girls today tell me similar stories, and sometimes it's worse. Being bullied for your beliefs is terrible, and that includes both vicious social media and face-to-face attacks. My heart goes out to them. But here's the thing. As I recovered from that ugly incident, a few people recognized me and offered words of support. "I'm glad you did that. I don't like McGovern either," they said. Unbeknownst to me, others had taken note and been emboldened, too. That's the way leadership works. And everyone can lead in some capacity.

All Shapes and Sizes

Just as many different instruments play together in an orchestra to create a single piece of music, girls of all backgrounds, strengths, and personalities can play a role in advancing the symphony of conservative ideas. Not everyone is cut out to be the next Phyllis Schlafly or Margaret Thatcher. We can't all be alpha women who take center stage and field the slings and arrows of our opponents. Some girls are shy and may be more effective behind the scenes. There is nothing wrong with that. The movement needs everybody. Parents can help by encouraging their daughter to step out of her comfort zone in accordance with her natural gifts. Campus activism is an opportunity to exercise a personal calling, and there is a buffet of options for getting involved.

Keep in mind that younger generations have developed differently. It seems every parent or grandparent has to tell young people how much harder they had it when they were coming up. But there is a noticeable trait in Millennials who were born from 1977 to 1996 and Generation Z young people born from 1997 on: when it comes to activism, many students lack initiative. They are much less willing to take risks. They have to be encouraged to get out and do things.

It's not their fault as much as it is the result of growing up with the internet. Hardly a moment passes when young adults aren't tethered to their smart phones. Selfies and social media are a vain distraction, but the real obstacle is Cancel Culture. Cancel Culture is defined as withdrawing or cancelling support for people or companies after they have done or said something the Left disagrees with. They are often cancelled on social media. Kids know what can happen if they are unlucky enough to be targeted by an online mob. Cyber bullying is nasty business, and keyboard cowards sometimes attack to get mob victims socially, academically, and professionally cancelled. You don't even have to do anything wrong. A false accusation or manipulated cell phone video can go viral and ruin a child's reputation before she even gets started in life.

It's unlikely that your daughter would ever face such abuse, but kids have seen it happen online, and the threat goes a long way towards creating a passive mindset. We all know the internet is forever. Imagine if the rugged individuals of the past matured with cameras filming their every move and naysayers posting harmful video clips to a public messaging board for all to see. They probably would have developed differently. It's a shame that something as productive as the internet can be weaponized against random people. But that's the age we live in, and it's all the more reason to support and applaud girls who engage in conservative activism.

Making a difference isn't easy, or everyone would do it. Fear is a powerful emotion, and the Left thrives on scaring people into silence. The threat of a media hit-piece or the high cost of Cancel Culture serves as a warning to anyone who doesn't toe the line. But parents should take heart. A more powerful motivation than fear is standing on principle and doing the right thing. It just takes courage. Good overcomes evil, and the consequences that come from standing up against injustice are a badge of honor. It's also likely to inspire others, which is how real political gains are made.

Parents can help motivate their daughter into action by appealing to her sense of service. Younger generations may be more passive when it comes to conservative activism, but they have other qualities that differentiate them from past generations. As a rule, younger people tend to be more committed to service; they far outshine the so-called "me" generation. It's an upside to online social connectivity. Girls are more exposed to different walks of life, and they are more apt to feel compassion as a result. Parents can tap into that wonderful impulse by explaining to their daughter that standing up for conservative principles helps other people. Sometimes it's easier to risk blowback when we are knowingly working on behalf of others and not just ourselves. In the words of Senator Barry Goldwater, "There is no greater service to this country than the defense of its freedom."

Bringing a Conservative Speaker to Campus

The number one activity for spreading conservative values on a college campus is to organize a speaker event. I know, because I have seen the results time and again. It's also what launched my passion to step into the arena of ideas back when I was in college. I got involved with Young Americans for Freedom and attended conferences with inspiring leaders. I met new people and was introduced to a new world of intellectuals and role models. The exposure helped solidify my confidence enough to start a chapter at my school.

Today, there are many, many brilliant women who carry the message and live their professed values with great influence. But in those days, there were virtually no nationally recognized conservative women. And my YAF "chapter"? I was the only member. So organizing a speaker event was a heavy lift, and pulling it off was so empowering that it unlocked my lifelong commitment to activism. The event didn't draw a huge crowd, yet it was lifechanging to put in the work and put myself out there for scrutiny. I sincerely hope your daughter has a similar experience.

Parents can encourage their daughter to take on this responsibility. There has never been more support for girls to lead a conservative lecture event than there is today, and the benefits are immense. I studied to be a teacher, but the experience made me want to spend my career promoting conservative ideas. It's a wonderful opportunity for girls to take initiative and to step into the fray, and the focus isn't all on them. Rather, they are taking a leadership position to bring in a role model to inspire others. Campus lectures definitely make a difference—not just for your daughter, but also for those who may never otherwise hear a conservative point of view at school.

Every intern who applies to the Clare Boothe Luce Center has to commit to organizing a live speaker event. That's how important it is. We train young women, we fund their events, and we support them through the process. We talk about who they want to bring and why. Again, parents can help their daughter by encouraging her to seek guidance from those who can assist her. It's so much more effective than writing an editorial for a school newspaper or arguing with a professor, although those are certainly good things. Organizing a lecture from start to finish makes young women understand that they can change the world around them. They change too, and they grow more deeply involved in the conservative movement.

Kimberly Martin Begg is a great example of what a difference organizing an event can make in a young girl's life. Kimberly has been active in the conservative movement since she attended her first YAF conference as a student at Rutgers University. Then, she worked for the YAF organization for nearly fifteen years, ascending to vice president and general counsel. She also oversaw YAF's legal department to protect students' free-speech rights on campus. Her first undergraduate speaker event at Rutgers was a lecture she organized with me at the Clare Boothe Luce Center. Kimberly recently told me that it changed her life. "It created a strong passion inside me," she said. "It lit a fire in me to be an activist for conservative ideas that I still have today."

I have two more stories about two young women whose lives were shaped by putting on a campus lecture. Both were born in Communist China and came to America as young girls with their families. Coming from a culture where women tend to be more reticent in public, they stepped forward to host speakers at key campuses where the Left was going crazy.

Jiesi Zhao is currently director of Gift Planning at UCLA. When she was an undergraduate at the University of California, Berkeley, she hosted a Phyllis Schlafly lecture before a crowd that barraged her with questions from a feminist perspective. Moving off the stage after she spoke, Schlafly tripped and fell, breaking her hip. In addition to all her work to put on the lecture, Jiesi showed great composure, tending to Mrs. Schlafly as emergency responders put her on a stretcher to take her to the hospital, notifying people, and making sure she was well cared for.

Jiesi went on to the University of Michigan Law School, started a student free enterprise program, and became an expert on school choice in a key Chicago organization. Jiesi said about the lecture, "I was determined to bring an alternative voice to campus," and said that Schlafly "...may have even inspired some of the students in attendance to think about women's rights from a different viewpoint—a perspective the students were never going to get from their professors." Jiesi noted, "In the midst of the chaos and considerable pain caused by her fall, Schlafly displayed the mental toughness and grace that has made her an inspiration to conservative women for generations."

Ying Ma was the communications director for Ward Connerly, president of the successful 2020 campaign "No on Prop 16." California voters rejected Proposition 16, an initiative that sought to restore racial preferences in college admissions. They won by 14 points, a resounding victory in a state that voted 2–1 the same election day for Joe Biden for president. Previously, she received her J.D. from Stanford University Law School and wrote *Chinese Girl in the Ghetto*, memoirs of her personal journey immigrating with her family from Communist China to the ghetto of Oakland, California, with its crumbling schools, unsafe streets, and scores of residents who were racist against the Chinese.

When Ying was an undergraduate at Cornell, she called me one day to ask for help bringing in a conservative woman speaker. She had to fight the usual Leftists to get it done but ended up having a good event. Now Ying lectures for the Clare Boothe Luce Center for Conservative Women and has told me many times how grateful she was for the help with the lecture and what a formative experience putting on a successful campus lecture was.

Ying later served in a key position in Ben Carson's presidential campaign and is an outstanding writer with frequently published articles on key policy issues, especially U.S.-China relations.

Without exception, girls who step out of the usual undergrad comfort zone, do all the work, and take on the responsibilities and challenges of putting on campus lectures move on to greater and extremely satisfying professional success in their lives.

In addition to personal growth and influencing other students, these events can also benefit liberal professors. Many will disagree with what they hear, but some may prioritize their intellectual curiosity over their politics. This presents an opportunity. College campuses are left-leaning to be sure, but not everyone is a radical feminist. Unlike modern, tribal Leftist activists, some old-school liberals can maintain the ability to engage across ideological lines. Your daughter can help stimulate good-faith debate by introducing conservative experts who would normally get short shrift. If she doesn't, who will? This goes back to Goldwater's notion that defending freedom is a public service, and I would argue that freedom desperately needs defending at universities.

We all know that the University of California, Berkeley, is about as radical as a campus community gets in the United States. Well, we had a young woman, a Luce Center summer intern named Victoria, who developed a positive academic relationship with a Berkeley professor during a public affairs class. She convinced him to allow her to have a Luce Center woman speaker give a conservative-oriented lecture in the tradition of hearing diverse points of view. It turns out she made an impression. Now this professor invites Luce to send conservative female speakers once or twice a year to his mandatory class of five hundred students, many of whom have never heard an actual conservative woman speak. It all started because Victoria identified an open-minded professor and took initiative.

Putting on a campus lecture is so important developmentally for a young woman. She learns how to deal with a relative celebrity—which most of the speakers are. The speaker has established herself professionally, so it shows your daughter how she might advance herself. It breaks the isolation of left-wing dominance on campus, which can be overwhelming and depressing. It gives her a lifelong contact with the speaker in Washington, D.C., in business, in the conservative movement, or wherever the speaker is from. The speaker can be a valuable contact for the rest of her days, in school and afterwards. And your daughter benefits from learning things from a conservative adult other than her parents.

Your daughter could do the same wherever she goes to school. Conservative organizations like the Clare Boothe Luce Center for Conservative Women will help with campus security costs, speaker travel expenses, and honoraria. There is no excuse not to host a lecture. Parents can help by encouraging their daughter to seek guidance and support opportunities to make a difference. She won't regret it.

Getting Connected

Speaker events are catalysts for change, but they are not the only way to get involved. The beauty of conservative activism is that there are virtually unlimited opportunities for girls to advance their principles in university settings where progressives and liberals dominate. Just being a known American Exceptionalist, for example, is an act of principled dissent. When your daughter knows her arguments, is prepared for debate, and has the courage to express her beliefs in appropriate moments, she is a force for change.

But girls need to go deeper. They need to organize and maintain a visual presence on campus. The good news is that much of the infrastructure they need to be successful either already exists or can be arranged through groups like the Clare Boothe Luce Center or Young Americans for Freedom. There are many outstanding people and organizations willing to help, but activism is ultimately self-initiated. It can also be fun.

We support female students who would like to experience a supervised trip to a gun range, for example. Rather than your typical "protest," putting beliefs into action is what activism is really all about, even if it's something new and exciting. Many college girls have never seen a gun before. They may be scared, which is completely understandable, or have preconceived notions. I was scared the first time I went to learn how to use a weapon and learn safety rules at a gun range. But what better way is there to teach them about firearm safety, self-defense, and their rights? They literally experience, as I did, the empowerment that comes from being able to protect themselves and their loved ones when police don't get there in time, as opposed to phony feminist empowerment schemes that turn girls into raving victims. If feminists are so worried about women's being treated as defenseless, dependent second-class citizens, then they should invest more energy in supporting the Second Amendment. It doesn't happen, because campus feminism is more about left-wing political advancement than anything else.

Parents should consider the amount of good that can come from such activities. Once a young woman uses a firearm in a controlled environment with a trained instructor, she is more likely to know the wisdom of the Founders on an issue that is demonized by college liberals and the news media. The negative stereotypes fall away, and your daughter may learn to question government intrusion in this area of her constitutional rights, if she hasn't already. Consider encouraging your daughter to join a group and invite a liberal friend to a fun excursion.

Another great activity is the annual March for Life rally in Washington, D.C., or one of the many local offshoots around the country. Girls can also volunteer to stage an event at their school. The March for Life is a massive pro-life celebration that brings people together for the sake of the unborn. It occurs every January, and there are many ways to participate. Attending a march with a group, promoting it at school and on social media, and looping in liberal friends could have a powerful impact. The Left keeps a stranglehold on the abortion issue within its ranks, so seeing sonogram pictures and learning about suppressed information like the relentless nature of abortion mills in African American communities has the potential to break through. Conservatives have made huge pro-life gains in recent years because of female activists speaking up for life!

Your daughter could also expose the happy, positive aspects of conservative activism to those who are unfamiliar with the movement. It never ceases to amaze me how activists differ on the left and right. We don't have violent extremists like Antifa's Marxists on our side. We have the Tea Party, which handed out pocket constitutions and picked up trash after their permitted protests. We don't riot, loot, deface historic statues, or spew venom at police officers. Campus Leftists used to spit at servicemen returning home from combat during the Vietnam War era, when I was an undergraduate from 1968 to 1972. That nastiness is unthinkable for conservatives, and your daughter could help highlight the divide by bringing friends to help them see and understand the differences. It's very persuasive. If radical feminists want to be miserable and act unhinged that's their business. Your daughter is entitled to have a great time advancing freedom and helping others experience the same.

Schedule Activities and Get Involved

One of the best ways to get going is to schedule a calendar of activist events. The March for Life is in January, so parents can remind their daughter about the annual pro-life celebration in advance and help her earn a trip to Washington, D.C. Parents can also encourage their daughter to connect with organized pro-life groups on campus and make posters, flyers, social media posts, and other supportive measures.

February is an opportunity to celebrate St. Valentine's Day. Parents might wonder who in the world doesn't like St. Valentine's Day. But they might be surprised to discover that feminists intentionally target the holiday because it represents traditional ideas about love, affection, marriage, romance, and beauty. Universities often host renditions of Eve Ensler's disgusting episodic play *The Vagina Monologues* in February as an unseemly rejection of wholesome values. It's a radical feminist extravaganza that I don't recommend for the faint of heart. Your daughter could take part in reclaiming the occasion by hosting an alternative event at her school or just openly celebrating the intellect, strength, integrity, and spirit of conservative women.

Each year, usually in February or early March, CPAC—the Conservative Political Action Conference—is held. I helped found this conference and get it started back in the 1970's. CPAC is not exactly like it used to be, where students dominated and hotels were lower-priced. It has become a bit more like a trade show, but the Luce Center has a presence at CPAC every year. CPAC is still an excellent first-time introduction for many students to the wider conservative movement. Every year the Luce Center hears from young women who attended CPAC and want to become more involved with us, want help putting on a lecture or other campus event, want to apply for one of our internships, or just want to ask for help with more information on an issue important to them. Small and larger groups of students often travel together to CPAC from their schools' conservative clubs.

March is Women's History Month. It's outrageous how the contributions and concerns of conservative women are filtered out of the annual history campaign. It's as if we don't exist. But as happy warriors, girls can take advantage of the opportunity instead of shrugging their shoulders and claiming victimhood. I'm reminded of what the great conservative pundit Charles Krauthammer once said about the juggernaut success of Fox News. He said the genius of Fox was that it served an untapped niche market in news broadcasting—half the American people.

There is no reason why conservative girls can't serve underrepresented students during Women's History Month. Parents can encourage their daughter to get involved by planning a week of highlighting different conservative women. Every year the Luce Center puts out a beautiful "Great American Conservative Women" calendar with photos and quotes each month from twelve women leaders who are involved with us. There are so many, yet they are unlikely to see the light of day unless student activists take the initiative to promote our great conservative ladies. Their efforts would almost certainly enlighten their classmates. Your daughter could also conduct a video project with interviews and reactions of others once they learn of the incredible achievements of conservative women throughout history. Girls can further hold events that debunk common myths like the wage gap, while showing how traditional women are thriving in society.

September is a chance to memorialize the heroes and victims of the September 11, 2001, terrorist attacks. There was so much bravery amid such a terrible tragedy. And many of our best and brightest men and women volunteered to join the military and do something about it. Why not take the opportunity to champion them? Your daughter could help organize a Support the Troops week and collect care-package items and thank-you cards to send to active military members serving overseas. She could hand out flyers and place posters around campus to commemorate the 9/11 Project. These activities could also bridge into serving veterans, especially around Veterans Day in November.

Before the close of the fall semester in December, make sure your daughter wishes everyone on campus a Merry Christmas and Happy

Hanukkah. It's amazing how those words can ruffle liberal feathers. Encourage your daughter to incorporate the meaning of Christmas into her classroom conversations and assignments. And if she really wants to go for it, tell her to send a Merry Christmas greeting card from her campus club group to the American Civil Liberties Union.

Girls can also remain active over the summer months by preparing for leadership roles in upcoming semesters and putting their acquired knowledge to use by writing blog posts and news editorials. It's always good to write and share ideas, but summer break presents more time to do so. Becoming a published author has many benefits, including building your daughter's professional reputation. At a minimum, your daughter should engage a strong summer reading list. Parents can help their daughter apply for summer internships with organizations that can take her activism to a new level—while having fun, of course. The Luce Center offers paid Fall, Spring, and Summer internships for young women students who are leaders or want to be leaders at their college. We always receive more applications than we have slots, so competition is spirited.

When the new school year rolls around in August, parents can encourage their daughter to join a conservative group, if she hasn't already, and invite her friends. Another option is to start her own group. The Clare Boothe Luce Center can help through our "Luce Society" program. It's an initiative that organizes campus activities for conservative female students so they can facilitate open discussions, network, and become leaders on campus for conservative ideas. It's pretty simple. Female students let us know what activity they would like to be brought to their school, and we work together with them to organize the entire thing. All your daughter would need to do is help promote the event and bring people.

Luce Society activities empower female students to take their freedom into their own hands and meet other conservative women doing the same. Your daughter could host a conservative author for brunch and a book discussion. She could host a local professional woman to learn how conservative values and policies have helped her succeed. She could bring our public-speaking workshop to campus, which is designed to help female students become more confident when talking about conservative ideas. We can also train your daughter to go deeper into leadership roles in other groups where she can bring in Luce-sponsored speakers.

Campus activism is also effective when well-trained students are able to respond to controversial events at their schools. This type of engagement can lead to news interviews and broad-based notoriety for the conservative point of view. These situations are huge opportunities, and there is plenty of support to prepare girls for moments when their activism will pay off the most.

Activism Can Have Costs, and That's OK

Let's talk about risk. No parent wants his or her daughter to experience pain. Leadership is tough but rewarding. And it comes with a cost when you are doing it right. There are degrees of activism, as we have discussed, but the Left generally feels entitled to lash out regardless. Often, the perpetrators will have the tacit support of faculty members and the school administration. But that should not deter your daughter from doing what's right.

I would never encourage a female student to put her physical safety at risk. Nor would I ever encourage getting arrested. But insults, unfairness, and discrimination can be part of the process. Parents should talk about risk and reward with their daughter and remind her that nothing of value comes easily. Let me describe a worst-case scenario:

One of our interns was "tabling," or standing at a table on campus with brochures, flyers, and other materials about her conservative club's policies and events. It's a relatively low-level form of activism, but it's important, and she had every right to be there. A group of about thirty angry students approached and started badgering her. That turned into screaming and throwing her materials onto the ground. She was terrified. People called her horrible names and falsely accused her of bad things, like racism. They made her cry. It was awful. It was wrong, and the aggressive students acted with impunity. Can you imagine the consequences if a large group of conservatives treated a feminist that way?

But the story doesn't end there. The young woman left the scene shaken and scared and sought the comfort of her friends and conservative confidants. She received unconditional care and support. And once she had moved through the experience, she became more determined. The young lady grew so resolved that she became a passionate activist, and she is now a chapter president for Young Americans for Freedom and is active with the Luce Center. The lesson is that bullies and thugs only win if we quit or silence ourselves. Yes, the brave female student was accosted, and I would never wish that on anyone. But she grew as an activist, leader, and woman as a result of how she handled it. She became more confident and braver. Now, she's inspiring other young women.

Professors are also known to take cheap shots. But girls should be encouraged to hold their heads high while picking and choosing their battles. One intern described how a particular professor would single her out because of her views. He would call on her and expect her to defend against his prejudices, as if she spoke for all conservatives. Another intern shared how she was mistreated for what she wrote in a college paper. The assignment was to write about something she was passionate about, so she spent hours and hours crafting a paper on abortion. It was 99 percent fact-based. Only the last paragraph directly revealed her personal position on the issue. But that was enough to receive a low grade. When the student attempted to discuss the problem with the professor, he berated her for being pro-life.

These things happen. They are ugly and unfair. But girls who press on anyway, especially those who stand up and fight with grace, gain a sense of accomplishment. Girls grow when they face adversity and remain true to themselves. Encourage your daughter to accept risk. Tell her to make the effort, and watch her reap the rewards, even if they come in spite of a bad experience. It's just like the children's song says: "This little light of mine, I'm gonna let it shine." It's a recipe for a life well-lived.

The Left wants to shield female students with safe spaces and suppression of alternative views. This is an implicit admission of intellectual failure. What parents need to teach their daughter is that some things are worth fighting for. Tell your daughter to use good judgment and that you support her no matter what. Let her know that standing up for her beliefs is honorable. In some cases, the costs may be too high. Not acting in those situations is smart. Again, girls should not put their physical safety at risk, but they should be trained for vigorous debate and be prepared for nasty behavior. Parents are sometimes harder to convince because they don't want their beautiful little girl to be targeted. I completely understand. But young, strong women can handle it. Interestingly, young women aren't typically as worried about what could go wrong as their parents. They tend to see the here and now. And with support, they can do amazing things.

Seizing the Day

College activism isn't something that is normally associated with conservatives. But campus activism isn't just for feminists. There are many ways for girls to get involved, and everyone can play a part according to her gifts. An array of groups and individuals is waiting to help.

Organizing a conservative speaker event is a powerful form of activism. Not only do accomplished women voice ideas that are generally unspoken at many colleges, but girls are empowered through the process of putting together these events. Planning a calendar of activities and being prepared to respond to school controversies are other effective means of advancing conservatism and bring more students into the fold.

Edmund Burke said, "All that is necessary for evil to triumph is for good [women] to do nothing."

There will be risks, but there is greater risk for their future if they do nothing. Parents can communicate the value of standing up for what's right. Hiding in fear is not the answer. Activism requires courage, and so does freedom. There's no better place for young women to engage than in universities. They are ground zero for the culture wars, as they mold young minds and release waves of new recruits into society every year. And politics, of course, is downstream from culture. Conservatives have ceded this fertile ground for too long. Now, parents can help by encouraging their daughter to stand up and make a difference.

CHAPTER 10

Communication Skills Are Key

Career survey after career survey shows that communications skills—both oral and written—are among the top traits employers seek. There's a reason for this: communication involves everything a person does, in one form or another. Even when a person is silent, she is still communicating nonverbally. So, if your daughter can't help but communicate throughout her life, she might as well learn to do it properly. Skillfully sending and receiving messages is also paramount for competing on the battlefield of ideas, where effecting change hinges on whether your daughter can effectively make her points and persuade others.

If she is presented with misleading information at school, the ability to explain the truth of the matter can be a powerful way to influence her peers. If a professor or a group of college feminists attempts to browbeat young women into agreeing with their agenda, standing up to them not only requires courage, but also the capacity to make meaningful counterarguments. Your daughter may know the truth in the moment, but without the skills to voice her views she is at the mercy of those who can. Like a child who can't quite get the words out, frustrated and disappointed students are prone to go silent and give up. That's why it's so important for conservative girls to be strong communicators.

If there is one specialized skill a conservative girl must master, it is communication. At the Clare Boothe Luce Center, we offer deep and rigorous training to help conservative girls learn how to effectively articulate the message of freedom, debate Leftists, craft powerful prose in the form of opinion articles and position papers, prepare for radio and TV appearances, and message across social media. Whether your daughter is planning a career in public service or just wants to gain confidence in sharing her conservative principles, strengthening her communication skillset will serve her well throughout her life and career.

Research Policy Facts and Know Your Topic

A brilliant moment occurred during the battle to confirm U.S. Supreme Court nominee, now justice, Amy Coney Barrett. Opposing Senate Judiciary Committee members peppered Barrett for hours on end over multiple days, often using false innuendo, rhetorical traps, crude assertions, and no-win questions to thwart her nomination. Hawaii senator Mazie Hirono even asked if Barrett had ever committed sexual assault, a loaded question that resembled the formulaic "have-you-stopped-beating-your-wife" trap. Answer yes, and you are, of course, guilty. Answer no, and you're on the defensive, where explaining and backpedaling looks like you're hiding something to those who are less inclined to give the benefit of the doubt. And either way, the answerer is cast in a suspicious light.

Hirono also pounced when Barrett uttered the phrase "sexual preference" during a well-reasoned response, as if the term sexual preference, rather than sexual orientation, was an admission of anti-homosexual prejudice. Like clockwork, the media ran with the insinuation, which fit the false narrative they had already laid. But throughout all the questioning and political games, Barrett had a command of the facts that none of the senators could match. It was her saving grace and her sword of truth.

At one point, Texas senator John Cornyn said, "You know, most of us have multiple notebooks and notes and books and things like that in front of us." "Hold up what you've been referring to in answering our questions," he said. Sitting alone at an empty table save for a single journal-sized booklet, Barret smiled while revealing a blank notepad. "Is there anything on it?" Cornyn pressed. "The letterhead. It says, 'United States Senate,'" she responded. The hearing room broke into laughter, and a few politicians were served a healthy portion of humble pie.

As a communicator, Judge Barrett had mastery over the facts. It made her untouchable. She didn't have to write anything down because she was so well prepared and knowledgeable about her subject matter. That is empowerment, and parents can encourage their daughter to research policy facts and learn chosen topics inside and out so that she is equipped with the sword and shield of knowledge. When she is the most informed person in the room, she will be a force others have to reckon with.

Parents can also help their daughter consider likely lines of counterattack to her conservative positions and help her defeat them through strong research and logic. Knowing anecdotes, illustrations, or famous quotations from history is also useful when debating a policy topic. Solely relying on data can lose connection with an audience—a way bean-counting fiscal conservatives often fall victim. In that case, it's helpful for your daughter to use an example or an expression to convey what she's trying to say. Think of how presidents use turns of phrase, historical appeals, and invited guests to highlight their policy goals during State of the Union speeches. It's what viewers remember the most. Even President Trump's media foes acknowledged the effectiveness of these tactics, such as when he honored a homeless veteran's road to recovery and a successful young woman who attributed her professional achievements to school choice.

Nonverbal Communication Matters

"An ounce of behavior is worth a pound of words," is a famous theatre expression that underscores the importance of nonverbal communication. It means gestures and movement can communicate in powerful ways. In fact, nonverbal behavior can communicate more than what is actually said. There's no such thing as silence when it comes to human interaction. Words are only one aspect of sending and receiving messages. Silence can say a lot, and body language expresses subtext that may be more revealing than dialogue.

Have you ever had a conversation with someone who started jiggling keys in his pocket? He may look you in the eyes and nod his head as if listening intently. But what he is really saying is that he wants to go. Maybe he's late for an appointment, or perhaps he has to use the bathroom. Even if you don't know the specifics, the general signal is clear. Tapping a foot, shifting toward the door, looking over your shoulder toward the clock, and biting one's lip—all of that behavior sends a message without uttering a single word. Most of the time we don't realize when we are doing it. Nor do we realize when we're picking up on someone else's nonverbal cues. It just happens. It makes us feel something, whether consciously or subconsciously, and then we make assumptions.

An instructive example of this happening in public policy occurred in the 1992 presidential campaign, when George H. W. Bush was seeking a second term in the White House. Bush stood on a debate stage next to then governor of Arkansas Bill Clinton and business magnate Ross Perot in a townhall setting. Ordinary Americans asked the candidates questions meant to represent working-class concerns—easy stuff for a skilled politician. But just before an audience member asked what the candidates would do to help economically struggling Americans, the TV cameras caught Bush looking down at his watch.

That single gesture was devastating to his reelection effort. It was terrible body language. Did he care about working Americans? Of course! But the image conveyed the impression that he didn't have time to care for regular folks; he had better things to do. His detractors ran with the idea and reinforced their caricature of a rich, out-of-touch, Ivy League patrician who thought more of getting away from the "common man" than listening to him. Bill Clinton, on the other hand, made it a habit to look directly into the cameras—as if he was looking the

American people in the eyes through their television screens—and saying, "I feel your pain," while giving the ol' thumbs up. And we all know how that turned out.

Eight years later, the tables turned when Al Gore committed a nonverbal faux pas. Gore was a skilled communicator who was locking horns with George W. Bush on the presidential campaign trail. During their first official debate, Gore sighed loudly into his microphone and rolled his eyes while Bush was talking. Many viewers got the impression that he was condescending and arrogant, a critique that still exists to this day. The point is that nonverbal communication matters because it shapes perception. Parents can help their daughter use this to her advantage and limit body language mistakes.

Let's explore some nonverbal dos and don'ts. First, strong posture communicates confidence. Leaders don't slouch or slump, and neither do empowered, graceful women. Standing up straight, shoulders resting at ease, chin in a normal position with your back and neck stretching to the sky while your hips and legs allow gravity to pull them into connection with the ground looks strong and feels good, too. Stand up, take a deep breath, and try it.

When sitting, women don't have as many options as men. Kicking up a leg and bending it over the opposing knee doesn't jibe with most female attire. Even though some of the Fox news ladies—especially when they are on high stools—do it to show their pretty legs on TV, that is because it's the desired Fox effect. For most women, to be a better communicator of your ideas, just don't do it in a public setting. However, elegant females always keep their shoulders back, their spines erect, and their heads held high. They also keep their legs together and use their arms to take up space. Generally, a woman presents herself better if she doesn't cross her arms, whether sitting or standing. Crossing one's arms suggests insecurity or uncertainty, whereas an "open" body posture with arms at your sides communicates acceptance, interest, and willingness to engage. It's an inviting position. Wouldn't you feel comfortable listening to someone who is sending a signal that they are open to you?

Hand gestures are also important. When using them, don't fidget or make distracting motions. Keep your palms open and facing your audience, as research indicates those who close their palms or hide their hands are perceived as less trustworthy. Placing a hand near or over the mouth is further perceived as a signal that the speaker is unsure of herself or lacking confidence in the accuracy of her statement. And when accuracy is compromised, whether in reality or perception, so is credibility. Finally, your daughter should avoid shuffling her feet or swaying when speaking. Distracting foot and body movements take the focus off what she is saying and put it on her shoes and body. She may be wearing a fabulous pair of shoes, but shoes are made for walking—not persuasive communication.

Mastering the Art of Public Speaking

An old joke asks, "How do you get to Carnegie Hall?" The answer? "Practice. Practice. Practice." And so it is with the art of public speaking.

As in anything else, some speakers have more natural ability than others. If your daughter is lucky enough to possess a rich voice, or if she has developed in a way that lends her to outwardly expressing herself, that's great. If not, that's fine, too. Giving a speech is a skill that anyone can learn if she does practice, practice, practice. No matter how much natural talent she was blessed with, your daughter will have to work diligently to hone her craft to be effective.

President Ronald Reagan was known as the "Great Communicator" because he had an incredible knack for connecting with the American people. But he also spent a lifetime speaking in the public eye. Before entering politics, Reagan was a radio sports announcer and Hollywood movie star. He knew the importance of memorizing lines and rehearsing them so that every word he uttered could be delivered as if he was saying it for the first time. That ethic carried over to his political career and was a huge advantage. Reagan used his rhetorical talents as a centerstage surrogate for Senator Barry Goldwater's presidential run, then as a two-term governor of California, and ultimately as the history-making president of the United States.

The irony of public speaking success is that you have to rehearse over and over again for your speech *not* to sound rehearsed. I know that personally; the very best speeches I have given have been ones I have practiced over and over. When our Luce Center interns and fellows are doing introductions for speakers at our events, I ask them to practice the introduction start to finish at least ten times in the bathroom mirror to become totally familiar with its content, to master the enunciation of the words, and to develop a rhythm to their presentation. Also, most women have to work on lowering their pitch and slowing down their delivery when speaking, and that takes a lot of practice too.

Girls should also work on eliminating "vocalized pauses" in their public speaking, or filler phrases like "um," "uh," "like...like...like," and "y'know?". Would you take someone seriously if she said "like" fifty times in a conversation, or "y'know" with an upward intonation at the end of every other sentence? Vocalized phrases aren't just hard on the ears, they undermine the speaker's credibility by making her seem ill-prepared.

The best technique to uproot filler words is a fun and silly exercise you and your daughter can do together. First, choose a word that you don't like the sound of. For example, the word "kumquat"—it just sounds weird. Next, any time your daughter uses a vocalized phrase during normal conversation, she must say the word out loud right in the middle of her sentence. This will be awkward and funny—a playful way to "punish" herself for using a filler phrase. It should sound something like this: "So yesterday during lunch, Cindy and I were, um...kumquat!...in the school cafeteria when we..." The point is that by raising her level of awareness she can begin to teach herself to catch and reduce her vocalized pauses.

Eye contact is also important. In fact, it reigns supreme. Why? Because eyes are the only soft tissue on the outside of the human body, and they connect to the brain, revealing what's inside. When we look someone in the eyes, it expresses sincerity, confidence, and command of our material. It gives the audience a sense of involvement and makes them *feel* what you are saying. It's a connection. Conversely, constantly looking down at one's notes suggests a lack of preparation or mastery of the material. The more your daughter practices, rehearses, and memorizes her talking points, the stronger her eye contact will be.

Thankfully, modern technology makes that easy. Almost every cell phone comes with a camera, so record your daughter practicing her speech and then review it with her. Allow her to pick out areas that she thinks could use improvement, then let her run through her address several more times to iron out the communication creases. Finally, record the session again, and let her see how she's improved and refined her performance. Consider repeating this exercise prior to her giving a speech or even for a brief presentation she might give in class or at a podium if there's time. It really helps the material sink in. Successful speaking experiences will help strengthen your daughter's confidence as a public communicator going forward.

Beating a Liberal in Debate

There is nothing worse than knowing you are right but being unable to articulate your position in an argument. The risk of embarrassment is enough to keep many girls silent, especially on college campuses where liberals have the luxury of having their politics and policy preferences as the default worldview of their community. Dare to think differently, and you are asking for trouble. This is also true in other areas of society, and the solution is rigorous debate prep. Your daughter will have to learn how to argue if she is to stand a fighting chance. Consider that good news. While liberals rest on their laurels, young conservative women can train for victory.

Our favorite Luce speaker to instruct students in how to engage in and win a debate with a liberal is President Ronald Reagan's U.S. treasurer, Bay Buchanan. In her talks to young women at Luce Center events over the years, Bay encourages young women to first pick an issue they really care about to firm up what they really believe and to learn everything they can about it. Bay often uses being pro-life as an example but says it would be the same with any issue.

Bay tells young women to seek out friends whom they know to be pro-choice and ask them why they believe what they believe. If things get a little heated, that's good. Their friends may raise points the young women don't know how to answer. This should lead them to read and learn more about the issue, maybe talk with someone who is more of an expert, maybe talk to someone who has had an abortion or someone who expresses the idea that there are two victims in an abortion. It should lead them to talk to more pro-choicers about life to court different opinions, incorporating what they learned in their conversations with others.

Bay's point is simple: when you get clobbered in an argument, that just means you are not well prepared yet. Everyone who engages in discussions on big issues has been there. There is no shame in this; it just means you need to do more reading and study and court more arguments.

Bay tells young women that by focusing on the false points that liberals make on a given topic, they will soon know far more than their liberal interlocutors. After just four or five encounters like this, a girl will know the lion's share of the talking points liberals deploy against conservatives. She will have learned how to craft arguments that respond to those points. In other words, she will know how to debate the issue with success. It may take time and effort, but the confidence it bestows is worth it. This is how a girl influences others and changes lives. If she sits back quietly with her beliefs, she will never be able to inspire others to change. People will try to intimidate and shame her. But by learning how to debate, a young woman will be harder to shake in her convictions. She will not be forced to back off or cower in the face of pressure.

Knowing the facts is critical, of course, but your daughter also needs to know how to navigate arguments if she is to be successful. This can be learned. All arguments rest on something rhetorical scholars call a "warrant"—the underlying assumption in a statement. It can be implied or explicit, and any facts or evidence offered in an argument support it. Exposing and nullifying an opponent's warrant is the key to winning any argument.

There are other logical fallacies your daughter can study and use to her advantage at an appropriate time. For example, a "straw man" argument is a classic tactic where the Left misrepresents a conservative position and then argues against it. "Conservatives don't like taxes because they would rather see poor people suffer than part with a little extra money. Well, that's just not right." Obviously, conservatives don't want poor people to suffer. Quite the opposite! We believe in limited government, a social safety net, that people should keep more of their own earnings, and that government is not effective at solving social problems. Often government's measures cause more harm. Period. By calling out straw man fallacies, your daughter will keep the upper hand in a debate.

Appealing to emotion is another favored debate tactic among Leftists. Instead of dealing in facts, they'll try to manipulate the emotions of their interlocutor. They might encourage listeners to dismiss a conservative argument by arousing fear, hatred, or disgust instead of offering evidence. An old legal expression comes to mind: "If the facts are against you, argue the law. If the law is against you, argue the facts. If the law and the facts are against you, pound the table and yell like crazy." Pounding and yelling encapsulate so much of how liberals interact with young conservatives. Calling it out for what it is is both an effective defense and offense in debate.

Other fallacies include ad hominem attacks, loaded questions, confirmation bias, slippery slope arguments, appeals to authority, and relying on anecdotal evidence to make broad claims. Help your daughter anticipate rhetorical tricks that liberals use against conservative beliefs and policy preferences. Then help her think through the chess moves regarding the best counterpoint responses. Learning to competently communicate will give your daughter confidence and the courage to speak up. She will also inspire others to join her.

Writing for Success

It's said that the pen is mightier than the sword, although these days the keyboard seems to be the weapon of choice. The meaning of the phrase still holds true: written communication is an effective tool for winning hearts and minds.

Your daughter doesn't have to be a great writer to be successful. She doesn't have to be the next Jane Austen, Ayn Rand, or J. K. Rowling. That's unrealistic. She only needs to develop strong writing skills to get her ideas across. This will not only benefit her in the here and now, but for the rest of her personal and professional life—while giving her more avenues through which to express her conservatism. Strong writing takes time and hard work. I'm sure your daughter is well on her way. But parents can help boost their daughter along by holding her to foundational principles.

The most important element to successful writing is clarity. Clear writing *is* strong writing; therefore clarity is king. Being too wordy, poorly organizing one's thoughts, conveying incomplete or inaccurate information, providing too much data, using wrong expressions, and having no clear point is not only torturous for readers, but it undermines the meaning one is trying to communicate.

Have your daughter begin by cutting unnecessary clutter words. This might be a little painful at first, as her 500-word homework assignment can quickly be whittled down to 400 words. But it will be stronger. Instead of writing, "She'll be back after a period of time." Cut it to, "She'll be back later." That's simple enough. Now, consider this wordy sentence: "Imagine someone trying to learn the rules for playing a game of chess." How much better it is to simply write, "Imagine learning chess." And so it goes. Always try to use fewer and more precise words to make your point.

Using passive voice, rather than active voice, is another common mistake for young writers. Passive voice occurs when the subject of a sentence is the recipient of the verb's action. For example, "The house was destroyed by the fire." Active voice, on the other hand, means the sentence has a subject that acts upon its verb, or, "The fire destroyed the house." In passive voice, the subject is always acted upon. "The lady was courted by the gentlemen." Whereas, active-voice sentences have a clear, direct, and forward-moving tone. It's essential for good writing. Ergo, "The gentlemen courted the lady."

It's also wise to keep adverbs and adjectives to a minimum, while using action verbs to make sentences sparkle. Adverbs are "-ly" words that attempt to spice up verbs but often do more harm than good. "She screamed loudly." Well, by definition, isn't screaming loud? "The girl looked at the boy flirtatiously." Ugh. Isn't it better to say she "batted her eyelashes"? Once your daughter understands adverbs and begins to cut them, she will know what Mark Twain meant when he said, "Adverbs are the tool of the lazy writer."

Adjectives play similar tricks. Young writers overuse them when attempting to energize their writing when they should use creative action verbs instead. Adjectives make sentences longer and more complicated. They serve to make prose prettier, but at what cost? It's not always bad, but misused adjectives might as well be typos. For example, "The girl went into a narrow alley." Well, aren't all alleys narrow? Of course they are. That's like saying "red stop signs" or "spherical baseballs." It's better to cut the adjective and say, "The girl entered the alley." However, adjectives are useful when they communicate something the noun cannot. "The girl went into a darkened alley." The word "darkened" tells the reader something unique and important. Now, consider employing creative action verbs. "The girl *slipped* into a darkened alley." "The girl *stumbled* into a darkened alley." "The girl *tiptoed* into a darkened alley." Action verbs communicate specificity and make writing fun.

These writing basics, and many other tricks of the trade, aren't mysteries reserved for the chosen few. Your daughter can find quality instruction online or in print. But she has to do the work if she wants to improve. Here are three great classics on the craft of writing every student should own and read: 1) Strunk & White's *Elements of Style*; 2) Roy Peter Clark's *Writing Tools: 55 Essential Strategies for Every Writer*; 3) William Zinsser's *On Writing Well: The Classic Guide to*

Writing Nonfiction. Using grammar software like Grammarly will help, too. Give your daughter the tools she needs to strengthen her communication skills. The rewards are great!

Putting It Together

Communication is constant. It's everything we do, whether spoken, written, or silent. The more skilled your daughter becomes at expressing herself, the more empowered she will be in life, as well as on the battlefield of ideas. Work with her. Encourage her. Get started today. The earlier she begins to learn public speaking and strong writing, the more effective she will be down the road. There is nothing better than expressing the truth of ourselves, especially when we are in conflict. At the Clare Boothe Luce Center, we understand this, and we are dedicated to teaching young women to communicate effectively, just as the courageous conservative women who came before us. It's a skill that will fling open a thousand doors throughout your daughter's life.

CHAPTER 11

Know the History of Great Conservative Women Leaders

Outstanding conservative women are rarely featured in a positive light, if they are discussed at all. Schools, colleges, women's studies courses, media, and popular culture either ignore or disparage them, despite their achievements benefitting all women. It's not fair, but can we do something about it? Yes, parents need to teach their daughters about great conservative women.

This chapter lists some incredible women whom you can acquaint your daughter with. Rest assured that it is unlikely she will hear anything positive about these ladies in school or the media. The list is by no means exhaustive, as there are countless conservative women who have opened doors and accomplished great things, including women on the Luce Center's board of directors and the many speakers who visit the Center and inspire young women at Luce Center summits, campus events, and mentoring lunches.

The following women are amazing leaders and role models for girls. Though I may sometimes disagree with them on particular issues, their dedication to conservative principles still merits praise. Take heart and know that your daughter comes from a long lineage of strong, graceful ladies, many of whom are fighting the good fight right now.

Clare Boothe Luce (1903–1987)
"The Preeminent Renaissance Woman of the Century" and Namesake of the Center for Conservative Women[1]

Clare Boothe Luce was one of the most acclaimed and accomplished women of the twentieth century. The Clare Boothe Luce Center for Conservative Women was founded in her honor, with the mission to prepare and promote conservative women leaders for generations to come. Many brilliant women were considered for the Center's name, but the choice was obvious.

A wife, mother, and woman of deep faith, Clare Boothe Luce launched her influential career at a time when few, if any, women were public leaders. She came from a broken home in which her father abandoned her family, and her homeschool education outweighed her two years of grammar school and two years of high school. Everything else in this amazing woman's life was self-taught.

Clare was a voracious reader throughout her life, with interests ranging from ancient philosophers to current affairs. She worked hard and sought mentors who emphasized discipline as a prerequisite to success. She studied topics and policies until she knew everything about them. Clare was brave beyond measure.

She blazed many trails for women. Clare became the editor of *Vanity Fair* magazine and took on great danger as a female journalist on the front lines in Europe and Asia during World War II. She was also an acclaimed author and playwright, a two-term U.S. congresswoman, and the first female ambassador appointed to a major nation when President Eisenhower dispatched her to Italy. These are extraordinary accomplishments for today's world, but they are stunning achievements for a gracious lady in the 1930s, 1940s, and 1950s.

At the tender age of twenty, Clare married a wealthy New Yorker whom her mother had recommended. Clare's first child, Ann Clare Brokaw, was born a year later. But by the time Clare was twenty-six, her husband had grown increasingly abusive and, by some accounts, violent. She was forced to leave him and turned to playwriting in 1934. Over the next six years, she wrote ten plays, four of which were produced and three of which became widely recognized successes.

In uncanny timing, Clare's lengthy interview with General Douglas MacArthur ran as the cover story in *Life* magazine on December 8, 1941, the day after the Japanese bombed Pearl Harbor. In one year alone, she logged 75,000 miles of air travel in her quest to report the events of World War II to American readers. By this time, she was an outspoken critic of President Franklin D. Roosevelt and his administration.

In 1942, Clare ran for Congress and won as a Republican representing a largely Democratic working-class district in Connecticut. But tragedy struck in the early morning hours of January 11, 1944, when her 19-year-old daughter Ann, who was driving from San Francisco to Stanford University after they visited together, was killed in a car accident. Clare was devastated. Prayer and religious devotion helped her cope with the terrible event. Notably, it was in the wake of the disaster that Bishop Fulton Sheen, the first televangelist and most eminent American Catholic churchman of the twentieth century, helped guide her to a celebrated conversion to Catholicism.

After extensive work on behalf of General Dwight D. Eisenhower's presidential bid, President Eisenhower appointed her U.S. ambassador to Italy. It was another landmark achievement for womankind, and the Italians came to admire her, respectfully naming her "la Signora," or the Lady. Her greatest diplomatic triumph came after eighteen months of bilateral negotiations with Yugoslavia and Italy, resulting in the Treaty of Trieste. Italy's oldest paper explained: "Perhaps never in the whole of history had a great nation owed so much to so small, fragile, and gentle a woman."

After returning home, Clare would serve on a variety of presidential advisory boards. She also received numerous public accolades and high honors, including the Congressional Distinguished Service Award and the Presidential Medal of Freedom, which was presented by President Ronald Reagan just before her eightieth birthday.

Clare Boothe Luce died at the age of 84 on October 9, 1987. She was living proof that women can succeed in America if they work hard and fight with grace. Her unique perspective is evident in her many famous quotes, such as:

"Courage is the ladder on which all other virtues mount."

"Because I am a woman, I must make unusual efforts to succeed. If I fail, no one will say, 'She doesn't have what it takes.' They will say, 'Women don't have what it takes.' "

"Thought has no sex. One either thinks, or one does not!" and especially,

"No good deed goes unpunished!"

Time magazine eulogized Clare Boothe Luce—wife, mother, writer, politician, diplomat, stateswoman—as "the preeminent Renaissance woman of the century." Indeed, she was.

Margaret Thatcher (1925–2013)

Britain's First Philosophically Conservative Prime Minister

From humble beginnings to the heights of power, Margaret Thatcher's life and legacy is a testament to conservative principles. Thatcher was born in a small town in eastern England where her family lived upstairs from their family grocery, where she worked growing up. She attended a local government school and excelled enough to earn a seat at Oxford University. There, she was elected student president of the school Conservative Association, and her journey to becoming the first woman to lead a major Western democracy was underway.[2]

Thatcher was elected British prime minister in 1979 and went on to win three successive general elections, a twentieth-century record. She moved swiftly upon taking office, saying, "I came to office with one deliberate intent: to change Britain from a dependent to a self-reliant society, from a give-it-to-me to a do-it-yourself nation."[3] Her vision to improve her country was based on the ideas of the conservative economists Friedrich von Hayek and Milton Friedman, namely that economic and political freedom are inseparable and that massive government spending distorts the natural strength of the marketplace.[4]

Thatcher's positions on social issues were also key to her leadership. She said, "Law and order *is* a social service. Crime and the fear which the threat of crime induces can paralyze whole communities, keep lonely and vulnerable elderly people shut up in their homes, scar young lives[,] and raise to cult status the swaggering[,] violent bully who achieves predatory control over the streets."[5] Those words ring true today.

She was a staunch supporter of women's rights but had no patience for left-wing feminists. Always one for wit, Lady Thatcher once quipped: "I hated those strident tones that you still hear from some women's libbers." Another famous Thatcher-esque line was "Being powerful is like being a lady. If you have to tell people you are, you aren't."[6]

She believed the United States was the world's foremost defender of liberty and partnered with President Reagan and Pope John Paul II to defeat the Soviet Union. Her achievements are nothing short of extraordinary. But her personal life was every bit as true to her principles. She married her husband, Denis, in 1951 and gave birth to twins two years later. Their marriage lasted more than 50 years until he passed.

Margaret Thatcher dedicated her life to serving Britain and the free world. She loved her family and was loyal to those around her. She is truly a tremendous role model for all women.

Phyllis Schlafly (1924–2016)
Conservative Icon Who Mobilized Millions of Proud Women to Defeat Radical Feminism and Champion America

Phyllis Schlafly was a highly accomplished woman who changed the course of American political history with humor, style, and fearlessness. She rose to prominence when women had few opportunities on the national stage, and she used her platform to give dignity to homemakers and other overlooked women.

Schlafly is best known for her leadership during a ten-year battle to defeat the Equal Rights Amendment, an unassuming name for the radical feminist movement's top legislative priority. Her success stemmed from motivating millions of ordinary women, including legions of stay-at-home moms who believed in classic American values but had no organized representation.

She became nationally recognized as a conservative force with the publication of her book *A Choice Not an Echo* in 1964. Schlafly wrote and edited twenty-seven books on a range of topics, including family, feminism, courts, religion, national defense, childcare, and education. She's credited along with Mildred Jefferson for making the Republican Party a pro-life party, which it remains today. She was a ferocious critic of radical feminism during the movement's cultural ascendence.

"The feminist movement is not about success for women," she said. "It is about treating women as victims and about telling women that you can't succeed because society is unfair to you, and I think that's a very unfortunate idea to put in the minds of young women because I believe women can do whatever they want."[7] She also said, "Self-imposed victimhood is not a recipe for happiness."[8]

Schlafly loved to tweak uptight feminists and to poke fun at liberal intolerance. She would open debates by saying, "I am only here today because my husband Fred said I could come." Schlafly was proud of her traditional family life, which included six children and a 44-year marriage. She never shied away from sharing her conservative beliefs.

A favorite speaker at the Clare Boothe Luce Center for Conservative Women, Schlafly was given its first-ever Lifetime Achievement Award in 2009. In her acceptance speech, she urged young women to believe that any one of them could become a leader with hard work. She stressed the destructive nature of the modern feminist movement and declared American women to be the most fortunate women who ever lived.

Dr. Mildred Fay Jefferson (1926–2010)
Early Right to Life Leader

Dr. Mildred Fay Jefferson was a passionate defender of life who broke countless glass ceilings. She grew up in Texas, graduated from high school at fifteen, earned a bachelor's degree at eighteen, and a master's degree in biology at twenty. Four years later, she became the first black woman to graduate from Harvard Medical School, then became the first female surgeon at Boston University Medical Center, where she also served as professor of surgery.[9]

Dr. Jefferson dedicated her life to medicine and protecting the unborn. "I became a physician in order to save lives, not to destroy them," she said, adding, "I will not accept the proposition that the doctor should relinquish the role of healer to become the new social executioner."[10]

Following the U.S. Supreme Court's *Roe v. Wade* decision, the petite Dr. Jefferson felt compelled by her Hippocratic oath to engage in public policy as a pro-life advocate. "When you believe something is wrong, you speak out," she said. "You wouldn't stand by on a cliff and watch somebody walk off.... We have to protect the weak and the helpless, the unborn."[11] She then became a founding member of National Right to

Life Committee and served as chairman of the board and president of the organization throughout the 1970s.

Dr. Jefferson called herself a "Lincoln Republican," and worked tirelessly for many pro-life candidates, including President Ronald Reagan. Her unwavering commitment to the unborn and her vast professional achievements made her a true pioneer for conservative women. For her, abortion was non-negotiable. "As a woman, I'm ashamed that the voices raised loudest in this demand to destroy the unborn children are those of other women. Blinded by an all-absorbing selfishness, these women are trying to force society to grant them rights without the responsibilities that our social contract demands, and privileges without the payment that our moral order commands."[12]

Dr. Mildred Jefferson pursued excellence and justice. She overcame early obstacles and worked her way to the top of her field, while never ceding her moral convictions. And Dr. Jefferson did it all with a smile on her face and a softness in her voice.

Frances Willard (1839–1898)
Seldom-venerated Suffragette Who Focused on Home and Family

Viewed through our 21st century feminist lens, women's achievements in the 1800s seem marginal. But that was not the case. Women's achievement at that time were nothing short of spectacular, in large part thanks to Frances Elizabeth Caroline Willard. "The nineteenth century is woman's century," she famously wrote with co-editor Mary A. Livermore. "Since time began, no other era has witnessed so many and so great changes in the development of her character and gifts and in the multiplication of opportunities for their application."[13]

Women today owe her a debt of gratitude—not that Women's Studies programs are keen to acknowledge her contributions. Frances Willard was an educator, writer, first Dean of Women at Northwestern

University, and a tireless women's rights advocate. She was also the president of the National Woman's Christian Temperance Union, which served as a springboard to advocate for a variety of social reforms to improve the lives of women and children. Willard used her platform to pursue a "do-everything" agenda that included suffrage. She was a "feminine feminist," and by 1890, Willard was "the second most well-known and influential woman in the world after Queen Victoria."[14]

Willard wisely and effectively introduced new, respectful home-and-family-centered arguments espousing female suffrage. She drew upon her Christian beliefs and saw women not as the helpless, dependent sex, but as partners with men in social and civic affairs. She argued that suffrage wasn't anti-men or anti-family. Rather, it was the "Home Protection Ballot." With the vote, women could better protect their homes and children, while greatly influencing society for the better.[15] It's not widely taught today, but she helped activate women in the home to pass the Nineteenth Amendment. They were critical to its success.

Frances Willard's life and work stands as a reminder to young women that they do not need to shed their femininity or desire to prioritize their home and family to achieve.

Abigail Adams (1744–1818)
Avid Defender of Women During the Early Years of the Republic

Abigail Adams was the wife of Founding Father and second U.S. president, John Adams, and mother of President John Quincy Adams. But there's no doubt that she deserves to stand alone in the annals of American history.

Though she was self-educated, Abigail Adams was a strong advocate for female education. She spent her life carefully advancing women's rights, and she pushed for the abolition of slavery. Abigail married John Adams at just nineteen years old and birthed six children. Home and family were her domain, as her husband spent many long periods away on business, even serving abroad in England and France.

She was intellectually curious and politically astute at an early age. Her father was a minister, farmer, and longtime speaker of the Massachusetts Assembly. A prodigious writer, Abigail worked behind the scenes on behalf of American women, often petitioning her own husband for change. In one famous letter published after her death, she urged him to apply "independence" to women as well as men during the Second Continental Congress in 1776:

> And, by the way, in the New Code of Laws which I suppose it will be necessary for you to make, I desire you would Remember the Ladies, and be more generous and favourable to them than your ancestors.... Remember all Men would be tyrants if they could. If particular attention is not paid to the Ladies we are determined to foment a Rebellion, and will not hold ourselves bound by any Laws in which we have no Voice, or Representation.[16]

Abigail Adams was a Founding Mother, who cared for her family, taught herself key policy issues of the day, and endeavored to help American women for all posterity. During its conception, the Clare Boothe Luce Center for Conservative Women nearly came to bear her name.

Saint Teresa of Calcutta (1910–1997)

Towering Religious Figure Who Dedicated Her Life to Serving Others.

Saint Teresa is truly a saint. Born Gonxha Agnes Bojaxhiu in Skopje, North Macedonia, (then part of the Ottoman Empire), she became a Roman Catholic nun who devoted her life to serving the poorest of the poor. "By blood, I am Albanian. By citizenship, an Indian. By faith,

I am a Catholic nun. As to my calling, I belong to the world. As to my heart, I belong entirely to the Heart of Jesus," she proclaimed.

At eighteen years old, she left her home to become a missionary, first in Ireland, then as a teacher in Calcutta, India. There, she established the religious community Missionaries of Charity and followed her calling to care for the sick, suffering, and truly destitute. She sent her Catholic sisters to serve other parts of India and inspired people around the world. "What can you do to promote world peace? Go home and love your family," she famously said.[17]

Her grace knew no bounds. Saint Teresa even touched the Clare Booth Luce Center for Conservative Women. In 2007, we were blessed to have an intern named Clare Girard, an undergraduate from Franciscan University who had planned to become a lawyer and dedicate her practice to saving babies from abortion. Clare had had the privilege of personally interacting with Saint Teresa. Her parents took her to a Mass for the Missionaries of Charity in New York when she was a baby, where Saint Teresa played with Clare and held her.

Her parents asked if she would pray that little Clare would become a missionary, to which Saint Teresa responded, "You pray!" But she later wrote letters to Clare's parents and invited them to pray that at least one of their children would commit to a life of service. After graduating college, Clare became a high school teacher. Then, one summer, her plans fell through, and she decided to travel to Kolkata (formerly Calcutta), India, to work as a summer volunteer with the Missionaries of Charity. Today, Sister Agnes Clare is teaching at Saint Rose Academy in Birmingham, Alabama.

Saint Teresa dedicated her life to loving and caring for others. She also influenced many, many women to do the same, including one special former intern at the Clare Boothe Luce Center for Conservative Women.

Ayn Rand (1905–1982)
Influential Author Who Popularized Economic Freedom with Her Brilliant Bestselling Novels

Ayn Rand is not a traditional conservative woman of faith and values, but no other woman has done more to promote capitalism and free enterprise in the popular imagination, while refuting the false promises of socialism. Millions upon millions of people in America and around the world have read her bestselling novels. They are mostly works of fiction, but her influence has greatly impacted real-world economics.

Ayn was born in Saint Petersburg, Russia. Her father's small business was confiscated following the 1917 Russian Revolution, and the event haunted her for the rest of her life. Ayn deeply resented communism. She fled to the United States in 1924 and soon after began writing. Ayn spent more than seven years crafting her first major book, *The Fountainhead*.

The story is a philosophical triumph of individualism over collectivism. It features a brilliant architect who was nearly destroyed for refusing to compromise his innovative vision with a threatened, disapproving establishment. Entrepreneurship, innovation, and creativity are what propel civilization forward, she argued. The "establishment," wherever one finds it, is what stands in the way. *The Fountainhead* was also made into a classic Hollywood film.

Her biggest success, *Atlas Shrugged*, was published in 1957 at nearly 1,200 pages. It's widely considered a masterpiece and continues to sell and influence readers to this day. The novel is both a lesson and warning. It depicts America on the verge of collapse due to socialist excess, where hard working, creative, and productive citizens are exploited by greedy incompetents who add no actual value to society. It's a dystopia that conservatives understand through the lens of out-of-control government and crony capitalism. True to form, *Atlas Shrugged* was attacked by political critics and those who preach envy and covetousness, who were outed for mooching off society.

CURRENT WOMEN LEADERS

Senator Marsha Blackburn
Most Prominent U.S. Senate Leader for Conservative Women's Views

A bold and gracious Southern lady, Senator Marsha Blackburn is a relentless defender of women and conservatism. She has inspired many, many people, especially young women, to work hard and fight for their values.

Senator Blackburn has always embraced challenges. She worked her way through college by selling books door-to-door, only after having persuaded the company to hire its first saleswoman. By the end of college, she had outperformed her competition despite unfair treatment and a full course load and rose to a sales manager position where men had to work for her. As she tells it, it was "truly stepping into the boys' club and changing the culture of the company."[18] That would become a theme throughout her life in business and government.

Senator Blackburn earned a special reputation as a leader and policy expert on telecommunications issues and intellectual property rights. She also became a trailblazer in the country music business, where she took to defending the rights of Nashville singers and songwriters in her home state of Tennessee. But Senator Blackburn saved the best of her fighting spirit for radical feminists and Washington, D.C., swamp politics.

During the U.S. Supreme Court confirmation hearings for Justice Amy Comey Barrett, Senator Blackburn took aim at those who targeted Justice Barrett for her personal—not judicial—beliefs: "They want to send a signal," she said. "If you're pro-life, pro-family, pro-religion, pro-business, pro-military, they do not think your voice counts—and if you're not in agreement with what the Left says should be women's issues."[19]

In her 2020 book, *The Mind of a Conservative Woman*, she explained, "...[T]he most prosperous and peaceful societies exist when government is kept in its boundaries, when markets are free, when individuals can rise as high as their gifts and character carry them, when faith is protected, when the protections of police and the military are mighty and principled, and when a culture of enterprise and innovation is encouraged."[20]

Senator Blackburn has spoken at many Clare Boothe Luce Center summits, luncheons, and seminars. She has appeared in the "Great American Conservative Women" calendar on numerous occasions and has supported the Center in many areas. In 2016, she was given the Clare Boothe Luce Center for Conservative Women's "Woman of the Year" award.

Kellyanne Conway

Senior White House Counselor and First Woman to Run a Successful Presidential Campaign in American History

In 2017, Kellyanne Conway received the Clare Boothe Luce Center's "Woman of the Year" award. She was a tremendous leader and had served on the Center's board of directors for seven years. But it was time to say goodbye. Kellyanne had just made history. She was the first female campaign manager since the nation's founding to lead a presidential campaign to victory. We were overjoyed at her success, and we understood, of course, that she was stepping down to serve as White House "Counselor to the President."

Kellyanne Conway is a brilliant woman. She's articulate and savvy and an expert polling analyst. She also possesses the rarest of traits in Washington, D.C.—common sense. Kellyanne grew up in New Jersey in a household full of women: her mother, grandmother, and two unmarried aunts. She was a high school valedictorian and excelled at choir and cheerleading. An all-American girl, she went on to graduate magna cum laude from Trinity College and earned a law degree from George Washington University.

Her talent for defeating liberals in debate and elections has frustrated feminists and media activists alike. Her formula is simple: she listens, then responds to left-wing attacks on conservative ideas with precision, accuracy, and grace. Despite her many achievements, including those that advanced the role of women in society, her political critics have levied reprehensible attacks against her and her family because of her conservative efficacy.

When Kellyanne left the White House in August 2020 to spend more time with her four children, which she called "less drama, more mamma," the vicious smears continued. One *Washington Post* "feminist" sneered at Kellyanne's "surrender to domesticity." She chalked up Kellyanne's incredible achievements this way: "There is absolutely zero need to feel sorry for Kellyanne. But she does make me feel...something. Some combination of awe and repugnance and confusion that she's spent so many of her obviously prodigious talents spinning stories for men who need their stories spun."

Like a true leader, Kellyanne shrugs off such petty jealousies. She's a role model for all women and a persistent, happy warrior for conservative principles, and America herself.

Governor Kristi Noem

Conservative Leader Who Dared to Protect Constitutional Freedoms during the COVID-19 Chinese Virus Pandemic

South Dakota governor Kristi Noem did the unthinkable during the COVID-19 Chinese virus lockdowns of 2020. She dared to protect constitutional freedoms, rather than trounce them like so many government officials. Governor Noem urged South Dakota residents and the American people not to give up their rights in the face of fear, but to take responsibility for their own health. Her approach to the pandemic was utterly American, but the blowback from the Left was deafening—and she didn't give an inch.

Noem may be the governor of a beautiful state, but she's also a wife, mother of three, lifelong rancher, and small business owner. She's an open Christian and a fervent believer in low taxes, limited government, and accountability. After multiple terms as the lone South Dakota congressional representative, Noem became the first elected woman governor in the state's history.

One of her specialties is confronting her left-wing critics with strength and grace. During the pandemic, she penned a *Wall Street Journal* editorial that helped pave the way for other public officials to resist harsh intrusions into citizens' private lives. "[South Dakota] hasn't issued lockdowns or mask mandates. We haven't shut down businesses or closed churches. In fact, our state has never even defined what an 'essential business' is. That isn't the government's role."[21]

When the media attacked her for allowing the Eightieth Annual Sturgis Motorcycle Rally to continue as scheduled, supposedly causing a so-called coronavirus "superspreader" event, Noem unspooled the phony science behind the attack.[22] "This report isn't science; it's fiction. Under the guise of academic research, this report is nothing short of an attack on those who exercised their personal freedom to attend Sturgis.... At one point, academic modeling also told us that South Dakota would have 10,000 COVID patients in the hospital at our peak. Today, we have less than 70. I look forward to good journalists, credible academics, and honest citizens repudiating this nonsense."[23]

Governor Noem is a governor who has the guts to stand up for the Constitution when it matters and the skill to beat the Left at its own games. She deserves credit for her courage, intelligent resolve, and fighting spirit.

Cleta Mitchell

Patriot, Campaign Finance Expert, and Political Law Attorney Who Exposed the Obama Administration's IRS Attacks on Conservatives

Cleta Mitchell has dedicated her life to defending the Constitution and victims of government abuse. She's constantly fighting to remind public officials that it is they who serve the American people, not the people who serve the government.

Her commitment to government accountability has led to countless legal victories. She even uncovered the truth about the extraordinary abuses the Obama administration and IRS unleashed against conservatives ahead of the 2012 presidential election. Cleta is a tireless woman of skill and grace who has never compromised her values in the face of "Deep State" intimidation. In 2013, the Clare Boothe Luce Center for Conservative Women named Cleta "Woman of the Year" during the Center's 20th Anniversary Dinner.

Cleta's legal career is full of achievement. She has represented numerous high-profile clients, including the National Rifle Association at the U.S. Supreme Court and True the Vote founder, Catherine Engelbrecht, during her multi-year battle with the IRS and other federal agencies.

Cleta served as legal counsel to the National Republican Senatorial Committee and the National Republican Congressional Committee. She sits on the board of directors of the Lynde and Harry Bradley Foundation and is chairman of the Public Interest Legal Foundation. She's also the past chairman of the American Conservative Union Foundation.[24]

Plus, Cleta doesn't just represent the abused; she's personally suffered, too. In 2018, she became "the target of a political and media smear" during the height of the Trump-Russia collusion hysteria. The *Wall Street Journal* editorial board explained: "The Russian collusion accusations ginned up by Fusion [GPS] at the behest of a law firm working for the Clinton campaign haven't been corroborated despite two years of investigations. But no one should forget the smears that they and their media mouthpieces peddled along the way."[25]

Dr. Laura Schlessinger

A Prolific "No-Nonsense" Talk Radio Host Who Stressed Personal Responsibility, Morality, and Traditional Values

Known simply as "Dr. Laura," Dr. Laura Schlessinger stepped firmly into the minds of American radio listeners for over forty years. She wrote numerous bestselling books and has reached a daily audience of 20 million people through more than 450 radio stations. And she did it with honesty, humor, and tough love. Rather than sell cheap, vulgar entertainment with shock-jock tactics, Dr. Laura made her mark by stressing personal responsibility, morality, and traditional values.

"My favorite kind of woman is a strong, confident woman. I groove, I resonate, with strong, confident women because they don't envy," she said in typical fashion.[26] On another occasion: "Our culture is horrible. Look at the meanness.... Human beings need restraint. That's why we have religion, we have rules, we have morality...."[27]

Dr. Laura was born in Brooklyn, New York, in 1947. She earned a Ph.D. in Physiology at Columbia University's College of Physicians and Surgeons and a postdoctoral certification in Marriage, Family, and Child Counseling from the University of Southern California. She also taught at USC and Pepperdine University before opening a successful private psychology practice. In 1975, she turned to radio, and the rest is history.

Callers would flood her AM radio show asking for help. Their stories were often riddled with the consequences of promiscuity and poor relationship decisions. A common response? "Girls, you need to keep your legs together!" She was anything but shy when it came to morals and values, which put her in the crosshairs of the Left. She was attacked by feminists, the homosexual community, and other liberals who called her "dangerous."

Dr. Laura received the Clare Boothe Luce Center's 2002 "Woman of the Year" award at a time when she was under vicious assault.

Today, she broadcasts not on AM radio but on Sirius XM radio and continues her mission to promote traditional values. Dr. Laura laughs at Cancel Culture, saying that "haters attempted to cancel her long before canceling became a vindictive verb."[28] Her desk nameplate sums up her philosophy succinctly: "GO, DO THE RIGHT THING."

Nonie Darwish

A Muslim-turned-Christian Who Lives under a Fatwa for Exposing Islamic Fundamentalist Abuses against Women.

In 2008, the Clare Boothe Luce Center for Conservative Women gave Nonie Darwish the "Woman of Exceptional Courage" award for her fearless and outspoken defense of Western freedom. A wife and mother or three, Nonie is an incredibly strong woman who has stood up for her beliefs and principles despite violent threats. She is considered a traitor by Islamists in her native country of Egypt, and a fatwa, or religious edict, was issued against her.

Born in Cairo in 1949, Nonie was raised a devout Muslim. She emigrated to the United States in 1976, and gradually converted to Christianity. That decision put her life at risk. But she chose to speak out and help other women who face many of the same obstacles she has overcome. "Ideology is everything," she has said. "It defines the culture that we live in, the standards by which we live."[29] She's also explained that "[i]n Islamic and socialists' systems, the head of State has no choice but to replace God, and citizens have no choice but to live under his mercy."[30]

Nonie has voiced frustration with American liberals, especially feminists, for their willingness to defend Islamic cultural abuses against women, which she came to the United States to escape. Why does the Western secular Left defend Islam when their professed values are so opposed?[31]

Writing for the American Thinker, Nonie blames many of society's modern problems on feminism and Leftists. Relentless social attacks against men, marriage, and family, she says, are a prime driver for chaotic inner-city home life, high crime, and conflict with police, who have the "impossible task of becoming the disciplinarian father figure that these young boys and girls never had."[32]

Star Parker

A Conservative Woman of Faith Who Rose Above Welfare, Abortion, and Drugs to Impact the Lives of Countless Women.

Star Parker is an incredible woman. She's an accomplished author, syndicated columnist, political activist, and campus lecturer who's spoken at more than 225 colleges since joining the conservative movement. Star's personal testimony is awe-inspiring. After years of welfare dependency, abortions, and drugs, she became a conservative woman of faith. Star walks the walk. She's is a powerful example to millions of young women.

In 2012, the Clare Boothe Luce Center for Conservative Women gave Star our Leadership Award for her courage and determination in promoting conservative values and for speaking out against the Left's harmful big-government, socialist policies. Rarely will you hear a more ferocious defender of freedom and faith. As an African-American woman, she's also an outspoken critic of the progressive attempt to bury the Civil Rights Movement and turn it into something it was never meant to be—anti-American.

"Liberals...don't want eternal truths that apply equally to all. And they certainly don't want personal responsibility to be the hallmark of individual behavior in a free country. They want a politicized nation where politicians gain power by making huge promises paid for by other people's money. And they want to make sure that if someone's life is not working, they can blame it on someone else," she wrote.[33]

Star has discussed her life before and after her conversion with stunning honesty. She had four abortions within three years and decided to see through her fifth pregnancy. She says welfare programs, unreported income, and selling medical vouchers helped her buy drugs and fare better "than working an honest 40-hour week."[34] But three black men planted the seeds of faith that changed her life. Star rejected religion at first, but eventually took their invitation to attend church. There, she met other black Christians who helped her recover and begin a new life.

Today, Star advances faith, freedom, and compassion through the Center for Urban Renewal and Education (CURE), an organization she founded, whose mission is to "preserve, promote and protect Christianity, Capitalism, and our Constitution to improve culture, reduce government dependency, and to build race relations."

Conclusion

Congratulations. You are to be commended. Your commitment to raising a conservative daughter in a hostile and often toxic culture shows you are dedicated to purposeful parenting. As we've discussed, it's not easy. But nothing worth doing ever is. Your daughter is certainly worth the effort. Even if she doesn't appreciate it now, she will later.

Beyond the myriad concepts, tools, and tips I've offered throughout this book, I'd like to leave you with a few final words of encouragement. First, while there's no such thing as a perfect parent, there is such a thing as a perfect and holy God. The best parental decisions, values, and principles flow from and are seen in the way our heavenly Father loves his children. So, when in doubt, our default parental setting should be to return to the immutable and transcendent Judeo-Christian truths that shaped America's founding.

Along your daughter's journey, you will experience trials and triumphs. Just as it's important to extend grace and understanding to your daughter, so, too, must you do the same for yourself. Life is messy and unpredictable. Sometimes forces beyond our control come crashing in and disturb our pristine parenting plans. That's normal. Don't beat yourself up when your daughter makes disappointing choices or when the lessons you intended to teach don't seem to stick day-to-day. Parenting is a marathon, not a sprint. Lessons you think may have fallen on deaf ears may later take full bloom in your daughter's heart and actions. Remember: as long as you are instilling the core conservative pillars we've discussed and seeking teachable moments to reinforce them, your daughter will be far more likely to embrace them over time.

And that's the point: we as parents have to do the work.

Hollywood, Madison Avenue, the establishment media, and the Leftist forces fueling academic radicalism have zero interest in helping you raise a conservative, smart, free-thinking daughter who fights for her values and for America. Since 1993, I've been blessed to help girls and young women receive the resources, tools, and training they need through the Clare Boothe Luce Center for Conservative Women. We know what works. And it always starts in the home.

As my old boss Ronald Reagan said, "All great change in America begins at the dinner table." Quality time together spent having fun and guiding and teaching your daughter your family's values is the bedrock. It also makes for enduring and meaningful memories. So enjoy the adventure! Before you know it, your little girl will be packing up and heading off, equipped with the values and knowledge you've instilled in her heart and mind. Few things in your life will ever compare in importance.

Acknowledgments

As founder and president of the Clare Boothe Luce Center for Conservative Women, I've spent decades listening to young women. I've also talked with many of our supporters about their challenges raising a conservative daughter.

I thought it would be worthwhile to share what I've learned: why some young women mature into strong, smart conservatives while others live less traditional lives.

So, my first thanks go to the thousands of young women who shared their ideas, experiences, and family upbringing—interns, fellows, campus leaders, and attendees at our lunches, seminars, conferences, summits, and other events. I've learned so much from all these accomplished and brave young women who participated. I hope they will enjoy this book.

The tens of thousands of supporters who have funded our work with young women over the years are also owed my deepest gratitude, and I wish I could name them all. Some have said they were disappointed they didn't do more to influence the women among their loved ones; others shared how they have had success. These thoughtful, caring, great Americans have a heart for helping ensure that more young women will achieve the success and happiness in life that come from living by conservative principles. These supporters are responsible for saving and changing the lives of so many of the young ladies we have worked with, and they should feel great joy in that.

This book furthers the mission of the Luce Center's board of directors, who want to help young women lead successful lives. Each board member helped inspire me in different ways, including Kate Obenshain Keeler, Clare Luce, Darla Partridge, Sarah Rindlaub, Linda Teetz, Ursula Meese, Nicole Hoplin, and Camille Hart.

I want to especially thank Luce Center board member Marji Ross, former president and publisher of Regnery Publishing, for her initial encouragement when she was the head of Regnery. She encouraged me to share my insights in this book and gave crucial advice along the way.

I also want to thank my wonderful Luce Center colleagues for their forbearance as I wrote this book. Their sharing their knowledge and experiences was essential to what you have before you.

Luce Center policy director Lil Tuttle has been my soul mate since we served together on Virginia governor George Allen's State Board of Education thirty years ago. Lil is a writer and researcher I greatly admire. Her help and advice on this book were invaluable.

I'm grateful to Kimberly Begg for her advice on the "Defend Life" chapter. Burt Folsom, who was also advisor to my son Thomas Robinson when he was at Hillsdale College, gave me indispensable advice on key history books for young women to read in chapter three. RJ, Danny, Thomas, Ali, Josephine, Trey and Charlie Robinson, my sister Carol, and my brother Glenn played more of a part than they might ever know.

I'm thankful for my mother and father, especially for when at our dinner table they would advise us four siblings if our conversation went off track and we uttered a liberal platitude. They seemed to be aware of the shifting of the culture starting in the 1950s and 1960s. I remember that when President Johnson proclaimed, "We will take from the haves and give to the have-nots," lengthy family conversations ensued about how liberal thinking discourages hard work and encourages dependency. Thank you, Mother and Father. I will always be indebted to you for taking the time to educate us on fundamental principles.

I also want to thank Michelle Hall and Will Patrick for their help in researching, writing, and editing—they have a magical touch. There were many others who I hope will forgive me for not mentioning them by name. In so many different ways over the years, they have all helped me understand the key lessons of conservatism and why these need to be taught to our children.

Paul Choix, the book's editor at Regnery, has been good and straightforward to work with.

Tom Spence, Regnery's current publisher and president, is the father of four lovely daughters, two of whom have taken part in Luce Center programs. Tom was enthusiastic about the book from the beginning. I'm grateful to him for understanding the need for this book. He and his wonderful wife, Amy, personify the principles that are at the heart of this book.

I have received wonderful writing advice over the years from William F. Buckley Jr., Priscilla Buckley, Daniel Oliver, RJ Robinson, Carter Clews, and Richard Viguerie—all excellent writers. But I have never worked with anyone more helpful and skilled than Wynton Hall.

Wynton spent hours and hours with me in conversation, probing to help me clearly articulate my experience and beliefs and then convey them in strong, easily readable advice in the book.

Ron Robinson, my husband of forty-eight years, and I spent a tremendous amount of time at home after work many nights and on weekends, thrashing out the key ideas and experiences. He reviewed many drafts for me. He helped me ensure the book reflected my views. Over the decades Ron and I have both met with so many young women, in our home and in our offices, getting to know them and their families and how it was that they became such wonderful young role models. The book reflects the kind of advice and insights that could have helped Ron and me as we raised our family.

And I thank God for giving me the life I have, blessed by so many good and loving people. God willing, this book will strengthen his family.

Notes

Chapter 1: Self-Worth Flows from God, Not Government

1. Michael Tanner and Charles Hughes, *The Work Versus Welfare Trade-Off: 2013: An Analysis of the Total Level of Welfare Benefits by State* (Washington, D.C.: Cato Institute, 2013), www.cato.org/sites/cato.org/files/pubs/pdf/the_work_versus_welfare_trade-off_2013_wp.pdf; Michael Tanner, "When Welfare Pays Better than Work," Cato Institute, August 19, 2013, https://www.cato.org/commentary/when-welfare-pays-better-work.

Chapter 5: A Woman's Differences Are Her Strengths

1. Jill Reilly, "'I Almost Made a Horrible Decision': American Idol Reject Whose YouTube Lullaby to Her Daughter Has Now Launched Her Singing Career Reveals How She Nearly Aborted Her Baby," DailyMail.com, March 17, 2015, https://www.dailymail.co.uk/news/article-2998876/American-Idol-reject-lullaby-online-sensation-reveals-aborted-baby-starts-movement-parents-sharing-photos-children-never-existed.html.

Chapter 6: Defend Life

1. Planned Parenthood, *Annual Report 2018–2019: We Are Planned Parenthood*, 2019, https://www.plannedparenthood.org/uploads/filer_public/2e/da/2eda3f50-82aa-4ddb-acce-c2854c4ea80b/2018-2019_annual_report.pdf.
2. Pro-Choice America, *50: 50 Years of Fighting for Reproductive Freedom*, 2020, https://www.prochoiceamerica.org/wp-content/uploads/2020/04/FY2019-Annual-Report-Digital-Edition.pdf.
3. National Abortion Federation, "Financials: How Do We Spend Our Funds?" https://prochoice.org/about/financials/.

4. Bridget Rowman, “Roll Call: EMILY’s List Names 2020 House and Senate Targets,” https://www.emilyslist.org/news/entry/emilys-list-names-2020-house-and-senate-targets.
5. Lila Rose, “The Numbers That Show Planned Parenthood about Abortion, Not Women’s Health,” The Daily Signal, September 14, 2016, https://www.dailysignal.com/2016/09/14/the-numbers-that-show-planned-parenthood-about-abortion-not-womens-health/.
6. Centers for Disease Control and Prevention, “Understanding Pregnancy Resulting From Rape in the United States,” https://www.cdc.gov/violenceprevention/datasources/nisvs/understanding-RRP-inUS.html.
7. Planned Parenthood of Greater New York, “Planned Parenthood of Greater New York Announces Intent to Remove Margaret Sanger’s Name from NYC Health Center,” July 21, 2020, https://www.plannedparenthood.org/planned-parenthood-greater-new-york/about/news/planned-parenthood-of-greater-new-york-announces-intent-to-remove-margaret-sangers-name-from-nyc-health-center.
8. Planned Parenthood, *Annual Report 2018–2019*.

Chapter 7: Manage Money Early and Often

1. Kandist Mallett, “Biden’s Call for ‘Unity’ Doesn’t Square with United States History,” *TeenVogue*, November 20, 2020, https://www.teenvogue.com/story/biden-political-unity-myth.
2. Dan Crenshaw (@DanCrenshawTX), “Teen Vogue publishes oped that says we should abolish private property rights…along with those pesky police. Just wondering if anyone sees any issues with our next generation reading Marxist propaganda in popular teen magazines…?”, Twitter, August 6, 2020, 9:55 p.m., https://twitter.com/DanCrenshawTX/status/1291553502594863104.
3. Lydia Saad, “Soicalism as Popular as Capitalism among Young Adults in U.S.,” Gallup, November 25, 2019, https://news.gallup.com/poll/268766/socialism-popular-capitalism-among-young-adults.aspx.

Chapter 8: Service to Others Yields Self-Reliance

1. Dick Wirthlin, *The Greatest Communicator: What Ronald Reagan Taught Me about Politics, Leadership, and Life* (Hoboken, New Jersey: Wiley & Sons, 2004), 224.
2. Sarah Sparks, "Community Service Requirements Seen to Reduce Volunteering," *Education Week*, August 20, 2013, https://www.edweek.org/ew/articles/2013/08/21/01volunteer_ep.h33.html; Arthur A. Stukas, Mark Snyder, and E. Gil Clary, "The Effects of 'Mandatory Volunteerism' on Intentions to Volunteer," *Psychological Science* 10, no. 1 (1999): 59-64, http://www.jstor.org/stable/40063378.
3. "Build a Shoebox Online," Operation Christmas Child, Samaritan's Purse, https://www.samaritanspurse.org/operation-christmas-child/buildonline/.
4. "Angel Tree Christmas," Prison Fellowship, https://www.prisonfellowship.org/about/angel-tree/angel-tree-christmas/.
5. "Toys for Tots," Toys for Tots Foundation, https://www.toysfortots.org.

Chapter 11: Know the History of Great Conservative Women Leaders

1. "Clare Boothe Luce: A Legacy of Leadership from One of the Most Acclaimed and Accomplished Women of the 20th Century," Clare Boothe Luce Center for Conservative Women, https://cblwomen.org/wp-content/uploads/2019/10/CBL-Picto-Bio-4x6-booklet-web.pdf.
2. "Biography," Margaret Thatcher Foundation, https://www.margaretthatcher.org/essential/biography.asp.
3. "Speech to Small Business Bureau Conference," Margaret Thatcher Foundation, February 8, 1984, https://www.margaretthatcher.org/document/105617.
4. Joseph R. Gregory, "Margaret Thatcher, 'Iron Lady' Who Set Britain on New Course, Dies at 87," *New York Times*, April 8, 2013, https://www.nytimes.com/2013/04/09/world/europe/former-prime-minister-margaret-thatcher-of-britain-has-died.html.

5. Margaret Thatcher, *The Path to Power* (London: HarperCollins Publishers, 1995), 558.
6. "Being powerful is like being a lady. If you have to tell people you are, you aren't," Margaret Thatcher Quotes, GoodReads, https://www.goodreads.com/quotes/57583-being-powerful-is-like-being-a-lady-if-you-have.
7. Andrea Sachs, "Phyllis Schlafly at 84," *Time*, April 7, 2009, http://content.time.com/time/nation/article/0,8599,1889757,00.html.
8. Jone Johnson-Lewis, "Phyllis Schlafly Anti-Feminist Quotes," ThoughtCo., February 15, 2019, https://www.thoughtco.com/phyllis-schlafly-anti-feminist-quotes-4084041.
9. Dennis Hevesi, "Mildred Jefferson, 84, Anti-Abortion Activist, Is Dead," *New York Times*, October 19, 2010, https://www.nytimes.com/2010/10/19/us/19jefferson.html.
10. Radiance Foundation, "Trailblazer: Dr. Mildred Jefferson," YouTube, February 10, 2014, https://youtu.be/nxefrRccsbI; National Right to Life, "National Right to Life Remembers Dr. Mildred Jefferson," YouTube, June 23, 2011, https://youtu.be/UB30-QazcNg.
11. Otile McManus, "Dr. Jefferson and Her Fight against Abortion," *Boston Globe*, December 5, 1976, https://www.newspapers.com/image/?clipping_id=21530686&fcfToken=eyJhbGciOiJIUzI1NiIsInR5cCI6IkpXVCJ9.eyJmcmVlLXZpZXctaWQiOjQzNjYyMDA5MCwiaWF0IjoxNTk5MDc2NzM0LCJleHAiOjE1OTkxNjMxMzR9.-nc8E_ZLs190t10vnm7QE50sVTgmzL63yXpnRClaFrY.
12. Randy Alcorn, "Meet Dr. Mildred Jefferson, First Black Woman to Graduate from Harvard Medical School and a Passionate ProLife Advocate," Eternal Perspective Ministries, February 17, 2020, https://www.epm.org/blog/2020/Feb/17/dr-mildred-jefferson.
13. Frances E. Willard and Mary A. Livermore, eds., *A Woman of the Century* (Charles Wells Moulton, 1893; Internet Archive, October 27, 2006), https://archive.org/details/womanofthecentur002516mbp/page/n3/mode/2up.

14. "Social Reform," Frances Willard House Museum and Archives, Center for Women's History and Leadership, https://franceswillardhouse.org/frances-willard/social-reform-agenda/.
15. Lil Tuttle, "The Battle within the Women's Movement," Clare Boothe Luce Center for Conservative Women, https://cblwomen.org/the-battle-within-the-womens-movement/.
16. History.com editors, "Abigail Adams," History.com, October 27, 2009, https://www.history.com/topics/first-ladies/abigail-adams.
17. "Mother Teresa Quotes," GoodReads, https://www.goodreads.com/author/quotes/838305.Mother_Teresa.
18. Marsha Blackburn, *The Mind of a Conservative Woman* (Nashville, Tennessee: Worthy Books, 2020), 35.
19. Nicholas Rowan, "Barrett Avoids Staking Out Position on *Roe* as Abortion Highlights Supreme Court Hearings," *Washington Examiner*, October 14, 2020, https://www.washingtonexaminer.com/news/barrett-avoids-staking-out-position-on-roe-as -abortion-highlights-supreme-court-hearings.
20. Blackburn, *The Mind of a Conservative Woman* .1.
21. Kristi Noem, "South Dakota's Balanced Covid Response," *Wall Street Journal*, December 7, 2020, https://www.wsj.com/articles/south-dakotas-balanced-covid-response-11607381485.
22. Brittany Shammas, "'Worst Case' at Sturgis Rally Could Link Event to 266,000 Coronavirus Cases: Study," September 10, 2020, https://www.washingtonpost.com/health/2020/09/08/worst-case-scenerios-sturgis-rally-may-be-linked-266000-coronavirus-cases-study-says/.
23. "Governor Noem: Modeling Isn't Reality," *South Dakota State News*, https://news.sd.gov/newsitem.aspx?id=27259.
24. "Cleta Mitchell," Foley and Lardner, LLP, https://www.foley.com/en/people/m/mitchell-cleta (no longer available).

25. Editorial Board, "Anatomy of a Fusion Smear," *Wall Street Journal*, August 31, 2018, https://www.wsj.com/articles/anatomy-of-a-fusion-smear-1535757026.
26. Amy Wallace, "The Doctor Is Out...for Revenge," *Los Angeles Magazine*, February 1, 2011, https://www.lamag.com/longform/the-doctor-is-out-for-revenge/.
27. Salena Zito, "Dr. Laura's Lasting Truths," *Washington Examiner*, November 24, 2019, https://www.washingtonexaminer.com/opinion/columnists/dr-laura-schlessingers-lasting-truths.
28. Ibid.
29. Brandon Showalter, "Muslim-Turned-Christian Author of 'Wholly Different' Says Islam Is a 'Rebellion against the Bible," *Christian Post*, February 24, 2017, https://www.christianpost.com/news/muslim-turned-christian-author-wholly-different-islam-rebellion-against-bible.html.
30. Nonie Darwish, "The Squad: A New Culture in Town," *Geller Report*, July 20, 2019, https://gellerreport.com/2019/07/nonie-darwish-on-the-squad.html/.
31. Ibid.
32. Nonie Darwish, "The Police, Patriarchy and Feminism," *American Thinker*, July 7, 2020, https://www.americanthinker.com/articles/2020/07/the_police_patriarchy_and_feminism.html.
33. Star Parker, "Democrats Bury the Civil Rights Movement," Townhall, August 12, 2020, https://townhall.com/columnists/starparker/2020/08/12/democrats-bury-thecivil-rights-movement-n2574146.
34. Linda Piepenbrink, "Star Parker: A Star Is Reborn," Today's Christian Woman, *Christianity Today*, 1997, https://www.todayschristianwoman.com/articles/1997/july/7w4022.html.